Clarence Darrow's

Sentencing Speech in

State of Illinois v.

Leopold and Loeb

PEG **The Professional Education Group, Inc.**

12401 Minnetonka Boulevard
Minnetonka, Minnesota 55343

Foreword

In the annals of jurisprudential debate, no single subject has evoked more passion or prejudice than the debate over the death penalty. In contemporary legal history, the trial of Nathan Leopold and Richard Loeb provided the vehicle for Clarence Darrow's stirring denunciation of justice by death. His now classic closing statement, in one of the most celebrated trials of our time, also shows a true master of the courtroom dealing with the cynical media and the largely hysterical public-at-large as part of his master strategy in the case.

The trial of Leopold and Loeb opened on July 24, 1924. The defendants (19 and 18 respectively) were charged with the kidnapping and murder of fourteen year old Bobby Franks. Nathan Leopold, Jr. was the son of a Chicago millionaire. Richard Loeb was the equally privileged son of a vice president of Sears, Roebuck & Co.

Nathan Leopold had long envisioned the so-called "perfect crime" and he succeeded in persuading his friend Richard Loeb to assist him. Leopold's eye glasses were found near the boy's body and proved to be the clue that broke the case for the prosecution. Confronted with the evidence, the two admitted to kidnapping Bobby Franks; demanding a ransom of $10,000 for his safe return; and killing him in spite of the willingness of the boy's father to cooperate.

Media attention surrounding the case had whipped the public's opinion regarding its outcome to a frenzy. Following the defendants' confession, the state's attorney publicly declared, "I have a hanging case." When the trial

began, the afternoon paper headline read "Darrow Pleads for Mercy: Mobs Riot."

The great Darrow had been called to the defense, much to the consternation of his friends and acquaintances who believed that he may have "sold out." To cool the public perception that a so-called "million dollar defense" would be mounted, he arranged for his fee to be determined by a committee of the Chicago Bar Association. [Seventy-five thousand dollars was eventually agreed upon.] Darrow himself has stated that his primary motivation for accepting the case was the opportunity to forcefully express his views on capital punishment. Walter and Benjamin Bachrach, relatives of the Loeb's, assisted Darrow for the defense.

The prosecution team was lead by State's Attorney Robert E. Crowe, a former Cook County Circuit Court Judge. He was assisted by Thomas Marshall, Joseph P. Savage, John Scarboro and Milton D. Smith. John R. Caverly, Chief Justice of the Criminal Court of Cook County was on the bench.

In his first address to the bench, Darrow stunned the packed courtroom by pleading his clients guilty and requesting only an opportunity to offer evidence of the mental states of Leopold and Loeb at the time of the murder in the hope that it would mitigate the punishment. Darrow believed that any Cook County jury impaneled in the volatile atmosphere created by the press would vote to hang his teen-aged clients. His entire strategy, and his client's lives, depended upon the success of his impassioned argument to the bench.

The imposition of the death penalty as punishment for serious crime has been debated for centuries. The com-

plexity of issues and strong advocates for both perspectives almost certainly assures that the public and professional discussions surrounding it will continue. Regardless of the future, Darrow's unique and enviable style, as applied to the dynamic closing argument in this case, will remain a classic.

The following excerpt from the trial transcript is the summation that Darrow delivered on August 22, 1924. The prosecution's closing lasted two days. On September 10, 1924, Leopold and Loeb were sentenced to life imprisonment on the charge of murder and to ninety-nine years on the charge of kidnapping.

Irving Younger
March, 1988

Your Honor, it has been almost three months since the great responsibility of this case was assumed by my associates and myself. I am willing to confess that it has been three months of great anxiety—a burden which I gladly would have been spared excepting for my feelings of affection toward some of the members of one of these unfortunate families. This responsibility is almost too great for anyone to assume, but we lawyers can no more choose than the court can choose.

Our anxiety over this case has not been due to the facts that are connected with this most unfortunate affair, but to the almost unheard-of publicity it has received; to the fact that newspapers all over this country have been giving it space such as they have almost never before given to any case. The fact that day after day the people of Chicago have been regaled with stories of all sorts about it, until almost every person has formed an opinion.

And when the public is interested and demands a punishment, no matter what the offense, great or small, it thinks of only one punishment, and that is death.

It may not be a question that involves the taking of human life; it may be a question of pure prejudice alone; but when the public speaks as one man it thinks only of killing.

We have been in this stress and strain for three months. We did what we could and all we could to gain the confidence of the public, who in the end really control, whether wisely or unwisely.

It was announced that there were millions of dollars to be spent on this case. Wild and extravagant stories were freely published as though they were facts. Here was to be an effort to save the lives of two boys by the use of

money in fabulous amounts, amounts such as these families never even had.

We announced to the public that no excessive use of money would be made in this case, neither for lawyers nor for psychiatrists, nor in any other way. We have faithfully kept that promise.

The psychiatrists, it has been shown by the evidence in this case, are receiving a per diem, and only a per diem, which is the same as is paid by the State.

The attorneys, at their own request, have agreed to take such amount as the officers of the Chicago Bar Association may think is proper in this case.

If we fail in this defense it will not be for lack of money. It will be on account of money. Money has been the most serious handicap that we have met. There are times when poverty is fortunate.

I insist, Your Honor, that had this been the case of two boys of these defendants' ages, unconnected with families supposed to have great wealth, there is not a state's attorney in Illinois who would not have consented at once to a plea of guilty and a punishment in the penitentiary for life. Not one.

No lawyer could have justified any other attitude. No prosecution could have justified it.

We could have come into this court without evidence, without argument, and this court would have given to us what every judge in the city of Chicago has given to everybody in the city of Chicago since the first capital case was tried. We would have had no contest.

We are here with the lives of two boys imperiled, with the public aroused.

For what?

Because, unfortunately, the parents have money. Nothing else.

I told Your Honor in the beginning that never had there been a case in Chicago, where on a plea of guilty a boy under twenty-one had been sentenced to death. I will raise that age and say, never has there been a case where a human being under the age of twenty-three has been sentenced to death. And, I think I am safe in saying, although I have not examined all the records and could not—but I think I am safe in saying—that never has there been such a case in the state of Illinois.

And yet this court is urged, aye, threatened, that he must hang two boys contrary to precedents, contrary to the acts of every judge who ever held court in this state.

Why?

Tell me what public necessity there is for this.

Why need the state's attorney ask for something that never before has been demanded?

Why need a judge be urged by every argument, moderate and immoderate, to hang two boys in the face of every precedent in Illinois, and in the face of the progress of the last fifty years?

Lawyers stand here by the day and read cases from the Dark Ages, where judges have said that if a man had a grain of sense left and a child if he was barely out of his cradle, could be hanged because he knew the difference between right and wrong. Death sentences for eighteen,

seventeen, sixteen, and fourteen years have been cited. Brother Marshall has not done half his job. He should read his beloved Blackstone again.

I have heard in the last six weeks nothing but the cry for blood. I have heard from the office of the state's attorney only ugly hate.

I have heard precedents quoted which would be a disgrace to a savage race.

I have seen a court urged almost to the point of threats to hang two boys, in the face of science, in the face of philosophy, in the face of humanity, in the face of experience, in the face of all the better and more humane thought of the age.

Why did not my friend, Mr. Marshall, who dug up from the relics of the buried past these precedents that would bring a blush of shame to the face of a savage, read this from Blackstone:

"Under fourteen, though an infant shall be judged to be incapable of guile prima facie, yet if it appeared to the court and the jury that he was capable of guile, and could discern between good and evil, he may be convicted and suffer death."

Thus a girl thirteen has been burned for killing her mistress.

How this case would delight Dr. Krohn!

He would lick his chops over that more gleefully than over his dastardly homicidal attempt to kill these boys.

One boy of ten and another of nine years of age who had killed their companion were sentenced to death; and he of ten actually hanged.

Why?

He knew the difference between right and wrong. He had learned that in Sunday school.

Age does not count.

Why, Mr. Savage says age makes no difference, and that if this court should do what every other court in Illinois has done since its foundation, and refuse to sentence these boys to death, no one else would ever be hanged in Illinois.

Well, I can imagine some results worse than that. So long as this terrible tool is to be used for a plaything, without thought or consideration, we ought to get rid of it for the protection of human life.

My friend Marshall has read Blackstone by the page, as if it had something to do with a fairly enlightened age, as if it had something to do with the year 1924, as if it had something to do with Chicago, with its boys' courts and its fairly tender protection of the young.

Now, Your Honor, I shall discuss that more in detail a little later, and I only say it now because my friend Mr. Savage—did you pick him for his name or his ability or his learning?—because my friend Mr. Savage, in as cruel a speech as he knew how to make, said to this court that we pleaded guilty because we were afraid to do anything else.

Your Honor, that is true.

We have said to the public and to this court that neither the parents, nor the friends, nor the attorneys would want these boys released. That they are as they are. Unfortunate though it be, it is true, and those closest to them know per-

fectly well that they should not be released, and that they should be permanently isolated from society. We have said that, and we mean it. We are asking this court to save their lives, which is the least and the most that a judge can do.

We did plead guilty before Your Honor because we were afraid to submit our case to a jury. I would not for a moment deny to this court or to this community a realization of the serious danger we were in and how perplexed we were before we took this more unusual step.

I can tell Your Honor why.

I have found that years and experience with life tempers one's emotions and makes him more understanding of his fellow-man.

Why, when my friend Savage is my age, or even yours, he will read his address to this court with horror.

I am aware that as one grows older he is less critical. He is not so sure. He is inclined to make some allowance for his fellow-man. I am aware that a court has more experience, more judgement and more kindliness than a jury.

Your Honor, it may be hardly fair to the court; I am aware that I have helped to place a serious burden upon your shoulders. And at that, I have always meant to be your friend. But this was not an act of friendship.

I know perfectly well that where responsibility is divided by twelve, it is easy to say: "Away with him."

But, Your Honor, if these boys hang, you must do it. There can be no division of responsibility here. You can never explain that the rest overpowered you. It must be

by your deliberate, cool, premeditated act, without a chance to shift responsibility.

It was not a kindness to you. We placed this responsibility on your shoulders because we were mindful of the rights of our clients, and we were mindful of the unhappy families who have done no wrong.

Now, let us see, Your Honor, what we had to sustain us. Of course, I have known Your Honor for a good many years. Not intimately. I could not say that I could even guess from my experience what Your Honor might do, but I did know something. I knew, Your Honor, that ninety unfortunate human beings had been hanged by the neck until dead in the city of Chicago in our history. We would not have civilization except for those ninety that were hanged, and if we cannot make it ninety-two we will have to shut up shop. Some ninety human beings have been hanged in the history of Chicago, and of those only four have been hanged on the plea of guilty—one out of twenty-two.

I know that in the last ten years four hundred and fifty people have been indicted for murder in the city of Chicago and have pleaded guilty. Four hundred and fifty have pleaded guilty in the city of Chicago, and only one has been hanged! And my friend who is prosecuting this case deserves the honor of that hanging while he was on the bench. But his victim was forty years old.

Your Honor will never thank me for unloading this responsibility upon you, but you know that I would have been untrue to my clients if I had not concluded to take this chance before a court, instead of submitting it to a poisoned jury in the city of Chicago. I did it knowing that

easier if their names are Richard and Nathan, so we will call them Richard and Nathan.

Eighteen and nineteen years old at the time of the homicide.

Here are three officers watching them. They are led out and in this jail and across the bridge waiting to be hanged. Not a chance to get away. Handcuffed when they get out of this room. Not a chance. Penned in like rats in a trap. And for a lawyer with a psychological eloquence to wave his fist in front of their faces and shout "Cowardly!" does not appeal to me as a brave act. It does not commend itself to me as a proper thing for a state's attorney or his assistant; for even defendants not yet hanged have some rights with an official.

Cold-blooded? Why? Because they planned, and schemed, and arranged and fixed?

Yes. But here are the officers of justice, so-called, with all the power of the state, with all the influence of the press, to fan this community into a frenzy of hate; with all of that, who for months have been planning and scheming, and contriving and working to take these two boys' lives.

You may stand them up on the trap door of the scaffold, and choke them to death, but that act will be infinitely more cold-blooded, whether justified or not, than any act that these boys have committed or can commit.

Cold-blooded!

Let the State, who is so anxious to take these boys' lives, set an example in consideration, kindheartedness and tenderness before they call my clients cold-blooded.

I have heard this crime described—this most distressing and unfortunate homicide, as I would call it; this cold-blooded murder, as the State would call it.

I call it a homicide particularly distressing because I am defending.

They call it a cold-blooded murder because they want to take human lives.

Call it what you will.

I have heard this case talked of, and I have heard these lawyers say that this is the coldest-blooded murder that the civilized world has ever known. I don't know what they include in the civilized world. I suppose Illinois. Although they talk as if they did not. But we will assume Illinois. This is the most cold-blooded murder, says the State, that ever occurred.

Now, Your Honor, I have been practicing law a good deal longer than I should have, anyhow for forty-five or forty-six years, and during a part of that time I have tried a good many criminal cases, always defending. It does not mean that I am better. It probably means that I am more squeamish than the other fellows. It means neither that I am better nor worse. It means the way I am made. I cannot help it.

I have never yet tried a case where the state's attorney did not say that it was the most cold-blooded, inexcusable, premeditated case that ever occurred. If it was murder, there never was such a murder. If it was robbery, there never was such a robbery. If it was a conspiracy, it was the most terrible conspiracy that ever happened since the Star Chamber passed into oblivion. If it was larceny, there never was such a larceny.

Now, I am speaking moderately. All of them are the worst. Why? Well, it adds to the credit of the state's attorney to be connected with a big case. That is one thing. They can say:

"Well, I tried the most cold-blooded murder case that ever was tried, and I convicted them, and they are dead," or:

"I tried the worst forgery case that ever was tried, and I won that. I never did anything that was not big."

Lawyers are apt to say that.

And then there is another thing, Your Honor: Of course, I generally try cases to juries, and these adjectives always go well with juries; bloody, cold-blooded, despicable, cowardly, dastardly, cruel, heartless—the whole litany of the state's attorney's office generally goes well with a jury. The twelve jurors, being good themselves, think it is a tribute to their virtue if they follow the litany of the state's attorney.

I suppose it may have some effect with the court; I do not know. Anyway, those are the chances we take when we do our best to save life and reputation.

"Here, your clients have pleaded guilty to the most cold-blooded murder that ever took place in the history of the world. And how does a judge dare to refuse to hang by the neck until dead two cowardly ruffians who committed the coldest-blooded murder in the history of the world?"

That is a good talking point.

I want to give some attention to this cold-blooded murder, Your Honor.

Was it a cold-blooded murder?

Was it the most terrible murder that ever happened in the state of Illinois?

Was it the most dastardly act in the annals of crime?

No.

I insist, Your Honor, that under all fair rules and measurements, this was one of the least dastardly and cruel of any that I have known anything about.

Now, let us see how we should measure it.

They say that this was a cruel murder, the worst that ever happened. I say that very few murders ever occurred that were as free from cruelty as this.

There ought to be some rule to determine whether a murder is exceedingly cruel or not.

Of course, Your Honor, I admit that I hate killing, and I hate it no matter how it is done—whether you shoot a man through the heart, or cut his head off with an ax, or kill him with a chisel or tie a rope around his neck. I hate it. I always did. I always shall.

But there are degrees, and if I might be permitted to make my own rules I would say that if I were estimating what was the most cruel murder, I might first consider the sufferings of the victim.

Now, probably the State would not take that rule. They would say the one that had the most attention in the newspapers. In that way they have got me beaten at the start.

But I would say the first thing to consider is the degree of pain to the victim.

Poor little Bobby Franks suffered very little. There is no excuse for his killing. If to hang these two boys would bring him back to life, I would say let them hang, and I believe their parents would say so, too. But:

The moving finger writes, and having writ,

Moves on; nor all your piety nor wit

Shall lure it back to cancel half a line,

Nor all your tears wash out a word of it.

Robert Franks is dead, and we cannot call him back to life. It was all over in fifteen minutes after he got into the car, and he probably never knew it or thought of it. That does not justify it. It is the last thing I would do. I am sorry for the poor boy. I am sorry for his parents. But it is done.

Of course I cannot say with the certainty of Mr. Savage that he would have been a great man if he had grown up. At fourteen years of age I don't know whether he would or not. Savage, I suppose, is a mind reader, and he says that he would. He has a fantasy, which is hanging. So far as cruelty to the victim is concerned, you can scarce imagine one less cruel.

Now, what else would stamp a murder as being a most atrocious crime?

First, I put the victim, who ought not to suffer; and next, I would put the attitude of those who kill.

What was the attitude of these two boys?

It may be that the state's attorney would think that it was particularly cruel to the victim because he was a boy.

Well, my clients are boys, too, and if it would make more serious the offense to kill a boy, it should make less serious the offense of the boys who do the killing.

What was there in the conduct of these two boys which showed a wicked, malignant and abandoned heart beyond that of anybody else who ever lived? Your Honor, it is simply foolish.

Everybody who thinks knows the purpose of this. Counsel knows that under all the rules of the courts they have not the slightest right to ask this court to take life. Yet they urge it upon this court by falsely characterizing this as being the cruelest act that ever occurred. What about these two boys—the second thing that would settle whether it was cruel or not?

Mr. Marshall read case after case of murders and he said: "Why, those cases don't compare with yours. Yours is worse." Worse, why? What were those cases? Most of his cases were robbery cases—where a man went out with a gun to take a person's money, and shot him down. Some of them were cases where a man killed from spite and hatred and malice. Some of them were cases of special atrocities, most connected with money. A man kills someone to get money, he kills someone through hatred. What is this case?

This is a senseless, useless, purposeless, motiveless act of two boys. Now, let me see if I can prove it. There was not a particle of hate, there was not a grain of malice, there was no opportunity to be cruel except as death is cruel—and death is cruel.

There was absolutely no purpose in it all, no reason in it all, and no motive for it all.

Now, let me see whether I am right or not.

I mean to argue this thoroughly, and it seems to me that there is no chance for a court to hesitate upon the facts in this case.

I want to try to do it honestly and plainly, and without any attempt at frills or oratory; to state the facts of this case just as the facts exist, and nothing else.

What does the State say about it?

In order to make this the most cruel thing that ever happened, of course they must have a motive. And what, do they say, was the motive?

Your Honor, if there was ever anything so foolish, so utterly futile as the motive claimed in this case, then I have never listened to it.

What did Tom Marshall say?

What did Joe Savage say?

"The motive was to get ten thousand dollars," say they.

These two boys, neither one of whom needed a cent, scions of wealthy people, killed this little inoffensive boy to get ten thousand dollars?

First let us call your attention to the opening statement of Judge Crowe, where we heard for the first time the full details of this homicide after a plea of Guilty.

All right. He said these two young men were heavy gamblers, and they needed the money to pay gambling debts—or on account of gambling.

Now, Your Honor, he said this was atrocious, most atrocious; and they did it to get the money because they were gamblers and needed it to pay gambling debts.

What did he prove?

He put on one witness, and one only, who had played bridge with both of them in college, and he said they played for five cents a point.

Now, I trust Your Honor knows better than I do how much of a game that would be. At poker I might guess, but I know little about bridge.

But what else?

He said that in a game one of them lost ninety dollars to the other one.

They were playing against each other, and one of them lost ninety dollars?

Ninety dollars!

Their joint money was just the same; and there is not another word of evidence in this case to sustain the statement of Mr. Crowe, who pleads to hang these boys. Your Honor, is it not trifling?

It would be trifling, excepting, Your Honor, that we are dealing in human life. And we are dealing in more than that; we are dealing in the future fate of two families. We are talking of placing a blot upon the escutcheon of two houses that do not deserve it. And all that they can get out of their imagination is that there was a game of bridge and one lost ninety dollars to the other, and therefore they went out and committed murder.

But let us go further than that. Who were these two boys? And how did it happen?

On a certain day they killed poor little Robert Franks. I will not go over the paraphernalia, the letter demanding money, the ransom, because I will discuss that later in

another connection. But they killed him. These two boys. They were not to get ten thousand dollars; they were to get five thousand dollars if it worked, that is, five thousand dollars each. Neither one could get more than five, and either one was risking his neck in the job. So each one of my clients was risking his neck for five thousand dollars, if that had anything to do with it, which it did not.

Did they need the money?

Why, at this very time, and a few months before, Dickie Loeb had three thousand dollars in a checking account in the bank. Your Honor, I would be ashamed to talk about this except that in all apparent seriousness they are asking to kill these two boys on the strength of this flimsy foolishness.

At that time Richard Loeb had a three-thousand-dollar checking account in the bank. He had three Liberty Bonds, one of which was past due, and the interest on each of them had not been collected for three years. I said, had not been collected; not a penny's interest had been collected—and the coupons were there for three years. And yet they would ask to hang him on the theory that he committed this murder because he needed money.

In addition to that we brought his father's private secretary here, who swears that whenever he asked for it, he got a check, without ever consulting the father. She had an open order to give him a check whenever he wanted it, and she had sent him a check in February, and he had lost it and had not cashed it. So he got another in March.

Your Honor, how far would this kind of an excuse go on the part of the defense? Anything is good enough to dump into a pot where the public are clamoring, and

where the stage is set and where loud-voiced young attorneys are talking about the sanctity of the law, which means killing people; anything is good enough to justify a demand for hanging.

How about Leopold?

Leopold was in regular receipt of one hundred and twenty-five dollars a month; he had an automobile; paid nothing for board and clothes and expenses; he got money whenever he wanted it, and he had arranged to go to Europe and had bought his ticket and was going to leave about the time he was arrested in this case.

He passed his examination for the Harvard Law School, and was going to take a short trip to Europe before it was time for him to attend the fall term. His ticket had been bought, and his father was to give him three thousand dollars to make the trip.

Your Honor, jurors sometimes make mistakes, and courts do, too. If on this evidence the court is to construe a motive out of this case, then I insist that human liberty is not safe and human life is not safe. A motive could be construed out of any set of circumstances and facts that might be imagined.

In addition to that, these boys' families were extremely wealthy. The boys had been reared in luxury, they had never been denied anything; no want or desire left unsatisfied; no debts; no need of money; nothing.

And yet they murdered a little boy against whom they had nothing in the world, without malice, without reason, to get five thousand dollars each. All right. All right, Your Honor, if the court believes it, if anyone believes it—I can't help it.

That is what this case rests on. It could not stand up a minute without motive. Without it, it was the senseless act of immature and diseased children, as it was; a senseless act of children, wandering around in the dark and moved by some emotion that we still perhaps have not had the knowledge or the insight into life to understand thoroughly.

Now, let me go on with it. What else do they claim?

I want to say to Your Honor that you may cut out every expert in this case, you may cut out every lay witness in this case, you may decide this case upon the facts as they appear here alone; and there is no sort of question that these boys were mentally diseased.

I do not know, but I do not believe that there is any man who knows this case, who does not know that it can be accounted for only on the theory of the mental disease of these two lads.

The State says, in order to make out the wonderful mental processes of these two boys, that they fixed up a plan to go to Ann Arbor to get a typewriter, and yet when they got ready to do this act, they went down the street a few doors from their house and bought a rope; they went around the corner and bought acid; then went somewhere else nearby and bought tape; they went down to the hotel and rented a room, and then gave it up, and went to another hotel, and rented one there. And then Dick Loeb went to the hotel room, took a valise containing his library card and some books from the library, left it two days in the room, until the hotel took the valise and took the books. Then he went to another hotel and rented another room. He might just as well have sent his card with the ransom letter.

They went to the Rent-a-Car place and hired a car. All this clumsy machinery was gone through without intelligence or method or rational thought. I submit, Your Honor, that no one, unless he had an afflicted mind, together with youth, could possibly have done it.

But let's get to something stronger than that. Were these boys in their right minds? Here were two boys with good intellect, one eighteen and one nineteen. They had all the prospects that life could hold out for any of the young—one a graduate of Chicago and another of Ann Arbor; one who had passed his examination for the Harvard Law School and was about to take a trip to Europe, another who had passed at Ann Arbor, the youngest in his class, with three thousand dollars in the bank. Boys who never knew what it was to want a dollar; boys who could reach any position that was given to boys of that kind to reach; boys of distinguished and honorable families, families of wealth and position, with all the world before them. And they gave it all up for nothing, nothing! They took a little companion of one of them, on a crowded street, and killed him, for nothing, and sacrificed everything that could be of value in human life upon the crazy scheme of a couple of immature lads.

Now, Your Honor, you have been a boy; I have been a boy. And we have known other boys. The best way to understand somebody else is to put yourself in his place.

Is it within the realm of your imagination that a boy who was right, with all the prospects of life before him, who could choose what he wanted, without the slightest reason in the world would lure a young companion to his death, and take his place in the shadow of the gallows?

I do not care what Dr. Krohn may say; he is liable to say anything, except to tell the truth, and he is not liable to do that. No one who has the process of reasoning could doubt that a boy who would do that is not right.

How insane they are I care not, whether medically or legally. They did not reason; they could not reason; they committed the most foolish, most unprovoked, most purposeless, most causeless act that any two boys ever committed, and they put themselves where the rope is dangling above their heads.

There are not physicians enough in the world to convince any thoughtful, fair-minded man that these boys are right. Was their act one of deliberation, of intellect, or were they driven by some force such as Dr. White and Dr. Glueck and Dr. Healy have told this court?

There are only two theories: one is that their diseased brains drove them to it; the other is the old theory of possession by devils, and my friend Marshall could have read you books on that, too, but it has been pretty well given up in Illinois.

That they were intelligent and sane and sound and reasoning is unthinkable. Let me call Your Honor's attention to another thing.

Why did they kill little Bobby Franks?

Not for money, not for spite, not for hate. They killed him as they might kill a spider or a fly, for the experience. They killed him because they were made that way. Because somewhere in the infinite processes that go to the making up of the boy or the man something slipped, and those unfortunate lads sit here hated, despised, outcasts, with the community shouting for their blood.

Are they to blame for it? There is no man on earth who can mention any purpose for it all or any reason for it all. It is one of those things that happened; that happened, and it calls not for hate but for kindness, for charity, for consideration.

I heard the state's attorney talk of mothers.

Mr. Savage is talking for the mothers, and Mr. Crowe is thinking of the mothers, and I am thinking of the mothers. Mr. Savage, with the immaturity of youth and inexperience, says that if we hang them there will be no more killing. This world has been one long slaughterhouse from the beginning until today, and killing goes on and on and on, and will forever. Why not read something, why not study something, why not think instead of blindly shouting for death?

Kill them. Will that prevent other senseless boys or other vicious men or vicious women from killing? No!

It will simply call upon every weak-minded person to do as they have done. I know how easy it is to talk about mothers when you want to do something cruel. But I am thinking of the mothers too. I know that any mother might be the mother of a little Bobby Franks, who left his home and went to his school, and who never came back. I know that any mother might be the mother of Richard Loeb and Nathan Leopold, just the same. The trouble is, that if she is the mother of a Nathan Leopold or of a Richard Loeb, she has to ask herself the question:

"How came my children to be what they are? From what ancestry did they get this strain? How far removed was the poison that destroyed their lives? Was I the bearer of the seed that brings them to death?"

Any mother might be the mother of any of them. But these two are the victims. I remember a little poem that gives the soliloquy of a boy about to be hanged, a soliloquy such as these boys might make:

The night my father got me
His mind was not on me;
He did not plague his fancy
To muse if I should be
The son you see.

The day my mother bore me
She was a fool and glad,
For all the pain I cost her,
That she had borne the lad
That borne she had.

My father and my mother
Out of the light they lie;
The warrant would not find them,
And here, 'tis only I
Shall hang so high.

O let not man remember

The soul that God forgot,
But fetch the county sheriff
And noose me in a knot,
And I will rot.

And so the game is ended,
That should not have begun.
My father and my mother
They had a likely son,
And I have none.

No one knows what will be the fate of the child he gets or the child she bears; the fate of the child is the last thing they consider. This weary old world goes on, begetting, with birth and with living and with death; and all of it is blind from the beginning to the end. I do not know what it was that made these boys do this mad act, but I do know there is a reason for it. I know they did not beget themselves. I know that any one of an infinite number of causes reaching back to the beginning might be working out in these boys' minds, whom you are asked to hang in malice and in hatred and injustice, because someone in the past has sinned against them.

I am sorry for the fathers as well as the mothers, for the fathers who give their strength and their lives for educating and protecting and creating a fortune for the boys that they love; for the mothers who go down into the shadow of death for their children, who nourish them and care for them, and risk their lives, that they may live, who watch

them with tenderness and fondness and longing, and who go down into dishonor and disgrace for the children that they love.

All of these are helpless. We are all helpless. But when you are pitying the father and mother of poor Bobby Franks, what about the fathers and mothers of these two unfortunate boys, and what about the unfortunate boys themselves, and what about all the fathers and all the mothers and all the boys and all the girls who tread a dangerous maze in darkness from birth to death?

Do you think you can cure it by hanging these two? Do you think you can cure the hatreds and the maladjustments of the world by hanging them? You simply show your ignorance and your hate when you say it. You may here and there cure hatred with love and understanding, but you can only add fuel to the flames by cruelty and hate.

What is my friend's idea of justice? He says to this court, whom he says he respects—and I believe he does—Your Honor, who sits here patiently, holding the lives of these two boys in your hands:

"Give them the same mercy that they gave to Bobby Franks."

Is that the law? Is that justice? Is this what a court should do? Is this what a state's attorney should do? If the state in which I live is not kinder, more humane, more considerate, more intelligent than the mad act of these two boys, I am sorry that I have lived so long.

I am sorry for all fathers and all mothers. The mother who looks into the blue eyes of her little babe cannot help musing over the end of the child, whether it will be crowned with the greatest promises which her mind can

image or whether he may meet death upon the scaffold. All she can do is to rear him with love and care, to watch over him tenderly, to meet life with hope and trust and confidence.

Your Honor, last night I was speaking about what is perfectly obvious in this case, that no human being could have done what these boys did, excepting through the operation of a diseased brain. I do not propose to go through each step of this terrible deed—it would take too long. But I do want to call the attention of this court to some of the other acts of these two boys, in this distressing and weird homicide; acts which show conclusively that there could be no reason for their conduct.

Without any excuse, without the slightest motive, not moved by money, not moved by passion or hatred, by nothing except the vague wanderings of children, they rented a car, and about four o'clock in the afternoon started to find somebody to kill. For nothing.

They went over to the Harvard School. Dick's little brother was there, on the playground. Dick went there himself in open daylight, known by all of them. He had been a pupil there himself. The school was near his home, and he looked over the little boys.

Your Honor has been in these courts for a long time; you have listened to murder cases before. Has any such case ever appeared here or in any of the books? Has it ever come to the human experience of any judge, or any lawyer, or any person of affairs? Never once!

Ordinarily there would be no sort of question of the condition of these boys' minds. The question is raised only because their parents have money.

They first picked out a little boy named Levinson, and Dick trailed him around.

As I think of that story of Dick trailing this little boy around, there comes to my mind a picture of Dr. Krohn—for sixteen years going in and out of the courtrooms in this building and other buildings, trailing victims without regard to the name or sex or age or surroundings. But he had a motive, and his motive was cash, as I will show further. One was the mad act of a child; the other the cold, deliberate act of a man getting his living by dealing in blood.

Dick abandons that lead; Dick and Nathan are in the car, and they see Bobby Franks on the street, and they call to him to get into the car. It is about five o'clock in the afternoon, in the long summer days, on a thickly settled street, built up with homes, the houses of their friends and companions, known to everybody, automobiles appearing and disappearing, and they take him in the car—for nothing.

If there had been a question of revenge, yes; if there had been a question of hate, where no one cares for his own fate, intent only on accomplishing his end, yes. But without any motive or any reason they pick up this little boy right in sight of their own homes, and surrounded by their neighbors. They drive a little way, on a populous street, where everybody can see, where eyes may be at every window as they pass by. They hit him over the head with a chisel and kill him, and go on about their business, driving this car within a half a block of Loeb's home, within the same distance of Franks's home, drive it past the neighbors that they know, in the open highway, in broad daylight. And still men will say that they have a bright intellect, and, as Dr. Krohn puts it, can orient them-

selves and reason as well as he can, possibly, and that it is the sane act of sane men.

I say again, whatever madness and hate and frenzy may do to the human mind, there is not a single person who reasons who can believe that one of these acts was the act of men—of brains—that were not diseased. There is no other explanation for it. And had it not been for the wealth and the weirdness and the notoriety, they would have been sent to the psychopathic hospital for examination, and been taken care of, instead of the state demanding that this court take the last pound of flesh and the last drop of blood from two irresponsible lads.

They pull the dead boy into the back seat, and wrap him in a blanket, and this funeral car starts on its route.

If ever any death car went over the same route or the same kind of a route driven by sane people, I have never heard of it, and I fancy no one else has ever heard of it.

This car is driven for twenty miles. First down through thickly populated streets, where everyone knows the boys and their families, and has known them for years, till they come to the Midway Boulevard, and then take the main line of a street which is traveled more than any other street on the south side except in the Loop, among automobiles that can scarcely go along on account of the number, straight down the Midway through the regular route of Jackson Park, Nathan Leopold driving this car, and Dick Loeb on the back seat, and the dead boy with him.

The slightest accident, the slightest misfortune, a bit of curiosity, an arrest for speeding—anything would bring destruction.

For what? For nothing! The mad acting of the fool in King Lear is the only thing I know of that compares with it. And yet doctors will swear that it is a sane act. They know better.

They go down a thickly populated street through South Chicago, and then for three miles take the longest street to go through this city—built solid with business buildings, filled with automobiles backed upon the street, with streetcars on the track, with thousands of peering eyes; one boy driving and the other on the back seat, with the corpse of little Bobby Franks, the blood streaming from him, wetting everything in the car.

And yet they tell me that this is sanity; they tell me that the brains of these boys are not diseased. You need no experts; you need no X rays; you need no study of the endocrines. Their conduct shows exactly what it was, and shows that this Court has before him two young men who should be examined in a psychopathic hospital and treated kindly and with care.

They get through South Chicago, and they take the regular automobile road down toward Hammond. There is the same situation—hundreds of machines; any accident might encompass their ruin. They stop at the forks of the road, and leave little Bobby Franks, soaked with blood, in the machine, and get their dinner, and eat it without an emotion or a qualm.

Your Honor, we do not need to believe in miracles; we need not resort to that in order to get blood. If it were any other case, there could not be a moment's hesitancy as to what to do.

I repeat, you may search the annals of crime, and you can find no parallel. It is utterly at variance with every

motive and every act and every part of conduct that influences normal people in the commission of crime. There is not a sane thing in all of this from the beginning to the end. There was not a normal act in any of it, from its inception in a diseased brain, until today, when they sit here awaiting their doom.

But we are told that they planned. Well, what does that mean? A maniac plans, an idiot plans, an animal plans, any brain that functions may plan; but their plans were the diseased plans of the diseased mind. Do I need to argue it? Does anybody need more than to glance at it? Is there any man with a fair intellect and a decent regard for human life and the slightest bit of heart that does not understand this situation?

And still, Your Honor, on account of its weirdness and its strangeness and its advertising, we are forced to fight. For what? Forced to plead to this court that two boys, one eighteen and the other nineteen, may be permitted to live in silence and solitude and disgrace and spend all their days in the penitentiary, asking this court and the state's attorney to be merciful enough to let these two boys be locked up in a prison until they die.

What do they want? Tell me, is a lifetime for the young boys spent behind prison bars—is that not enough for this mad act? And is there any reason why this great public should be regaled by a hanging?

I cannot understand it, Your Honor. It would be past belief, excepting that to the four corners of the earth the news of this weird act has been carried and men have been stirred, and the primitive has come back, and the intellect has been stifled, and men have been controlled by feel-

ings and passions and hatred which should have died centuries ago.

My friend Savage pictured to you the putting of this dead boy in this culvert. Well, no one can minutely describe any killing and not make it shocking. It is shocking. It is shocking because we love life and because we instinctively draw back from death. It is shocking wherever it is and however it is, and perhaps all death is almost equally shocking.

But here is the picture of a dead boy, past pain, when no harm can come to him, put in a culvert, after taking off his clothes so that the evidence would be destroyed; and that is pictured to this court as a reason for hanging. Well, Your Honor, that does not appeal to me as strongly as the hitting over the head of little Robert Franks with a chisel. The boy was dead.

I could say something about the death penalty that, for some mysterious reason, the State wants in this case. Why do they want it? To vindicate the law? Oh, no. The law can be vindicated without killing anyone else. It might shock the fine sensibilities of the state's counsel that this boy was put into a culvert and left after he was dead, but, Your Honor, I can think of a scene that makes this pale into insignificance. I can think, and only think, Your Honor, of taking two boys, one eighteen and the other nineteen, irresponsible, weak, diseased, penning them in a cell, checking off the days and the hours and the minutes until they will be taken out and hanged. Wouldn't it be a glorious day for Chicago? Wouldn't it be a glorious triumph for the state's attorney? Wouldn't it be a glorious triumph of justice in this land? Wouldn't it be a glorious illustration of Christianity and kindness and charity? I can picture them, wakened in the gray light of morning, fur-

nished a suit of clothes by the State, led to the scaffold, their feet tied, black caps drawn over their heads, stood on a trap door, the hangman pressing a spring so that it gives way under them; I can see them fall through space—and—stopped by the rope around their necks.

This would surely expiate placing Bobby Franks in the culvert after he was dead. This would doubtless bring immense satisfaction to some people. It would bring a greater satisfaction because it would be done in the name of justice. I am always suspicious of righteous indignation. Nothing is more cruel than righteous indignation. To hear young men talk glibly of justice. Well, it would make me smile if it did not make me sad. Who knows what it is? Does Mr. Savage know? Does Mr. Crowe know? Do I know? Does Your Honor know? Is there any human machinery for finding it out? Is there any man who can weigh me and say what I deserve? Can Your Honor? Let us be honest. Can Your Honor appraise yourself, and say what you deserve? Can Your Honor appraise these two young men and say what they deserve? Justice must take account of infinite circumstances which a human being cannot understand.

If there is such a thing as justice it could only be administered by one who knew the inmost thoughts of the man to whom he was meting it out. Aye, who knew the father and mother and grandparents and the infinite number of people back of him. Who knew the origin of every cell that went into the body, who could understand the structure and how it acted. Who could tell how the emotions that sway the human being affected that particular frail piece of clay. It means more than that. It means that you must appraise every influence that moves men, the civilization where they live, and all society which enters

into the making of the child or the man! If Your Honor can do it—if you can do it you are wise, and with wisdom goes mercy.

No one with wisdom and with understanding, no one who is honest with himself and with his own life, whoever he may be, no one who has seen himself the prey and the sport and the plaything of the infinite forces that move man, no one who has tried and who has failed—and we have all tried and we have all failed—no one can tell what justice is for someone else or for himself; and the more he tries and the more responsibility he takes, the more he clings to mercy as being the one thing which he is sure should control his judgement of men.

It is not so much mercy either, Your Honor. I can hardly understand myself pleading to a court to visit mercy on two boys by shutting them into a prison for life.

For life! Where is the human heart that would not be satisfied with that?

Where is the man or woman who understands his own life and who has a particle of feeling that could ask for more? Any cry for more roots back to the hyena; it roots back to the hissing serpent; it roots back to the beast and the jungle. It is not a part of man. It is not a part of that feeling which, let us hope, is growing, though scenes like this sometimes make me doubt that it is growing. It is not a part of that feeling of mercy and pity and understanding of each other which we believe has been slowly raising man from his low estate. It is not a part of the finer instincts which are slow to develop; of the wider knowledge which is slow to come, and slow to move us when it comes. It is not a part of all that makes the best there is in man. It is not a part of all that promises any hope for the

future and any justice for the present. And must I ask that these boys get mercy by spending the rest of their lives in prison, year following year, month following month, and day following day, with nothing to look forward to but hostile guards and stone walls? It ought not to be hard to get that much mercy in any court in the year 1924.

These boys left this body down in the culvert, and they came back and telephoned home that they would be too late for supper. Here, surely, was an act of consideration on the part of Leopold, telephoning home that he would be late for supper. Dr. Krohn says he must be able to think and act because he could do this. But the boy who, through habit, would telephone his home that he would be late for supper had not a tremor or a thought or a shudder at taking the life of little Bobby Franks for nothing, and he has not had one yet. He was in the habit of doing what he did when he telephoned—that was all; but in the presence of life and death, and a cruel death, he had no tremor and no thought.

They came back. They got their dinners. They parked the bloody automobile in front of Leopold's house. They cleaned it to some extent that night and left it standing in the street in front of their home.

"Oriented," of course. "Oriented." They left it there for the night, so that anybody might see and might know. They took it into the garage the next day and washed it, and then poor little Dickie Loeb—I shouldn't call him Dickie, and I shouldn't call him poor, because that might be playing for sympathy, and you have no right to ask for sympathy in this world; you should ask for justice, whatever that may be; and only state's attorneys know.

And then in a day or so we find Dick Loeb with his pockets stuffed with newspapers telling of the Franks tragedy. We find him consulting with his friends in the club, with the newspaper reporters; and my experience is that the last person that a conscious criminal associates with is a reporter. He shuns them even more than he does a detective, because they are smarter and less merciful. But he picks up a reporter, and he tells him he has read a great many detective stories, and he knows just how this would happen and that the fellow who telephoned must have been down on Sixty-Third Street, and the way to find him is to go down to Sixty-Third Street and visit the drugstores, and he would go with him.

And Dick Loeb pilots reporters around the drugstores where the telephoning was done, and he talks about it, and he takes the newspapers, and takes them with him, and he is having a glorious time. And yet he is "perfectly oriented," in the language of Dr. Krohn. "Perfectly oriented." Is there any question about the condition of his mind? Why was he doing it? He liked to hear about it. He had done something that he could not boast of directly, but he did want to hear other people talk about it, and he looked around there and helped them find the place where the telephone message was sent out.

Your Honor has had experience with criminals and you know how they act. Was any such thing as this ever heard of before on land or sea? Does not the man who knows what he is doing, who for some reason has been overpowered and commits what is called a crime, keep as far away from it as he can? Does he go to the reporters and help them hunt it out? There is not a single act in this case that is not the act of a diseased mind, not one. Talk about scheming. Yes, it is the scheme of disease; it is the scheme

of infancy; it is the scheme of fools; it is the scheme of irresponsibility from the time it was conceived until the last act of the tragedy. And yet we have to talk about it, and argue about it, when it is obvious to anyone who cares to know the truth.

But they must be hanged, because everybody is talking about the case, and their people have money.

Am I asking for much in this case?

Let me see for a moment now. Is it customary to get anything on a plea of Guilty? How about the state's attorney? Do they not give you something on a plea of Guilty? How many times has Your Honor listened to the state's attorney come into this court, with a man charged with robbery with a gun, which means from ten years to life, and on condition of a plea of Guilty, ask to have the gun charge stricken out, and get a sentence of three to twenty years, with a chance to see daylight inside of three years? How many times? How many times has the state's attorney himself asked consideration for everything including murder, not only for the young, but even the old? How many times have they come into this court, and into every court, not only here but everywhere, and asked for it? Your Honor knows. I will guarantee that three times out of four in criminal cases, and much more than that in murder, ninety-nine times out of one hundred, and much more than that; I would say not twice in a thousand times has the state failed to give consideration to the defendant on a plea.

How many times has Your Honor been asked to change a sentence, and not hold a man guilty of robbery with a gun, and give him a chance on a plea of Guilty—not a boy but a man?

How many times have others done it, and over and over and over again? And it will be done so long as justice is fairly administered; and in a case of a charge of robbery with a gun, coupled with larceny, how many times have both the robbery and the gun been waived, and a plea of larceny made, so that the defendant might be released in a year?

How many times has mercy come even from the state's attorney's office? I am not criticizing. It should come and I am telling this court what this court knows. And yet forsooth, for some reason, here is a case of two immature boys of diseased mind, as plain as the light of day, and they say you can get justice only by shedding their last drop of blood!

Why? I can ask the question easier than I can answer it. Why? It is unheard of, unprecedented in this court, unknown among civilized men. And yet this court is to make an example or civilization will fail. I suppose civilization will survive if Your Honor hangs them. But it will be a terrible blow that you shall deal. Your Honor will be turning back over the long, long road we have traveled. You will be turning back from the protection of youth and infancy. Your Honor would be turning back from the treatment of children. Your Honor would be turning back to the barbarous days which Brother Marshall seems to love, when they burned people thirteen years of age. You would be dealing a staggering blow to all that has been done in the city of Chicago in the last twenty years for the protection of infancy and childhood and youth.

And for what? Because the people are talking about it. Nothing else. It would not mean, Your Honor, that your reason was convinced. It would mean in this land of ours, where talk is cheap, where newspapers are plenty, where

the most immature expresses his opinion, and the more immature the stronger, that a court couldn't help feeling the great pressure of the public opinion which they say exists in this case.

Coming alone in this courtroom with obscure defendants, doing what has been done in this case, coming with the outside world shut off, as in most cases, and saying to this court and counsel:

"I believe that these boys ought not to be at large; I believe they are immature and irresponsible, and I am willing to enter a plea of Guilty and let you sentence them to life imprisonment," how long do you suppose Your Honor would hesitate? Do you suppose the state's attorneys would raise their voices in protest?

You know it has been done too many times. And here for the first time, under these circumstances, this court is told that you must make an example.

Can you administer law without consideration? Can you administer what approaches justice without it? Can this court or any court administer justice by consciously turning his heart to stone and being deaf to all the finer instincts which move men? Without those instincts I wonder what would happen to the human race?

If a man could judge a fellow in coldness without taking account of his own life, without taking account of what he knows of human life, without some understanding—how long would we be a race of real human beings? It has taken the world a long time for man to get to even where he is today. If the law was administered without any feeling of sympathy or humanity or kindliness, we would begin our long, slow journey back to the jungle that was formerly our home.

How many times has assault with intent to rob or kill been changed in these courts to assault and battery? How many times has felony been waived in assault with a deadly weapon and a man or boy given a chance? And we are asking a chance to be shut up in stone walls for life. For life. It is hard for me to think of it, but that is the mercy we are asking from this court, which we ought not to be required to ask, and which we should have as a matter of right in this court and which I have faith to believe we will have as a matter of right.

Is this new? Why, I undertake to say that even the state's attorney's office—and if he denies it I would like to see him bring in the records—I will undertake to say that in three cases out of four of all kinds and all degrees, clemency has been shown.

Three hundred and forty murder cases in ten years with a plea of Guilty in this county. All the young who pleaded guilty, every one of them—three hundred and forty in ten years with one hanging on a plea of Guilty, and that man forty years of age. And yet they say we come here with a preposterous plea for mercy. When did any plea for mercy become preposterous in any tribunal in all the universe?

We are satisfied with justice, if the court knows what justice is, or if any human being can tell what justice is. If anybody can look into the minds and hearts and the lives and the origin of these two youths and tell what justice is, we would be content. But nobody can do it without imagination, without sympathy, without kindliness, without understanding, and I have faith that this Court will take this case, with his conscience, and his judgement and his courage and save these boys' lives.

Now, Your Honor, let me go a little further with this. I have gone over some of the high spots in this tragedy. This tragedy has not claimed all the attention it has had on account of its atrocity. There is nothing to that.

What is it?

There are two reasons, and only two that I can see. First is the reputed extreme wealth of these families; not only the Loeb and Leopold families, but the Franks family, and of course it is unusual. And next is the fact it is weird and uncanny and motiveless. That is what attracted the attention of the world.

Many may say now that they want to hang these boys; but I know that giving the people blood is something like giving them their dinner. When they get it they go to sleep. They may for the time being have an emotion, but they will bitterly regret it. And I undertake to say that if these two boys are sentenced to death and are hanged, on that day a pall will settle over the people of this land that will be dark and deep, and at least cover every humane and intelligent person with its gloom. I wonder if it will do good. I wonder if it will help the children—and there is an infinite number like these. I marveled when I heard Mr. Savage talk. I do not criticize him. He is young and enthusiastic. But has he ever read anything? Has he ever thought? Was there ever any man who had studied science, who has read anything of criminology or philosophy—was there ever any man who knew himself who could speak with the assurance with which he speaks?

What about this matter of crime and punishment, anyhow? I may know less than the rest, but I have at least tried to find out, and I am fairly familiar with the best

literature that has been written on that subject in the last hundred years. The more men study, the more they doubt the effect of severe punishment on crime. And yet Mr. Savage tells this court that if these boys are hanged, there will be no more murder.

Mr. Savage is an optimist. He says that if the defendants are hanged there will be no more boys like these.

I could give him a sketch of punishment—punishment beginning with the brute which killed something because something hurt it; the punishment of the savage. If a person is injured in the tribe, they must injure somebody in the other tribe; it makes no difference who it is, but somebody. If one is killed his friends or family must kill in return.

You can trace it all down through the history of man. You can trace the burnings, the boilings, the drawings and quarterings, the hanging of people in England at the crossroads, carving them up and hanging them as examples for all to see.

We can come down to the last century when nearly two hundred crimes were punishable by death, and by death in every form; not only hanging—that was too humane—but burning, boiling, cutting into pieces, torturing in all conceivable forms.

You can read the stories of the hangings on a high hill, and the populace for miles around coming out to the scene, that everybody might be awed into goodness. Hanging for picking pockets—and more pockets were picked in the crowd that went to the hanging than had been known before. Hangings for murder—and men were murdered on the way there and on the way home. Hangings for poaching, hangings for everything, and hangings in

public, not shut up cruelly and brutally in a jail, out of the light of day, wakened in the nighttime and led forth and killed, but taken to the shire town on a high hill, in the presence of a multitude, so that all might see that the wages of sin were death.

I know that every step in the progress of humanity has been met and opposed by prosecutors, and many times by courts. I know that when poaching and petty larceny were punishable by death in England, juries refused to convict. They were too humane to obey the law; and judges refused to sentence. I know that when the delusion of witchcraft was spreading over Europe, claiming its victims by the millions, many a judge so shaped his cases that no crime of witchcraft could be punished in his court. I know that these trials were stopped in America because juries would no longer convict. I know that every step in the progress of the world in reference to crime has come from the human feelings of man. It has come from that deep well of sympathy which, in spite of all our training and all our conventions and all our teaching, still lives in the human breast. Without it there could be no human life on this weary old world.

Gradually the laws have been changed and modified, and men look back with horror at the hangings and the killings of the past. What did they find in England? That as they got rid of these barbarous statutes, crimes decreased instead of increased; as the criminal law was modified and humanized, there was less crime instead of more. I will undertake to say, Your Honor, that you can scarcely find a single book written by a student—and I will include all the works on criminology of the past—that has not made the statement over and over again that

as the penal code was made less terrible, crimes grew less frequent.

Now let us see a little about the psychology of man.

If these two boys die on the scaffold—which I can never bring myself to imagine—if they do die on the scaffold, the details of this will be spread over the world. Every newspaper in the United States will carry a full account. Every newspaper of Chicago will be filled with the gruesome details. It will enter every home and every family.

Will it make men better or make men worse? I would like to put that to the intelligence of man, at least such intelligence as they have. I would like to appeal to the feelings of human beings so far as they have feelings—would it make the human heart softer or would it make hearts harder? How many men would be colder and crueler for it? How many men would enjoy the details? And you cannot enjoy human suffering without being affected for better or for worse; those who enjoyed it would be affected for the worse.

What influence would it have upon the millions of men who will read it? What influence would it have upon the millions of women who will read it, more sensitive, more impressionable, more imaginative than men? Would it help them if Your Honor should do what the State begs you to do? What influence would it have upon the infinite number of children who will devour its details as Dickie Loeb has enjoyed reading detective stories? Would it make them better or would it make them worse? The question needs no answer. You can answer it from the human heart. What influence, let me ask you, will it have for the unborn babes still sleeping in their mother's womb? And

what influence will it have on the psychology of the fathers and mothers yet to come? Do I need to argue to Your Honor that cruelty only breeds cruelty?—that hatred only causes hatred?—that if there is any way to soften this human heart, which is hard enough at its best, if there is any way to kill evil and hatred and all that goes with it, it is not through evil and hatred and cruelty; it is through charity, and love and understanding?

How often do people need to be told this? Look back at the world. There is not a man who is pointed to as an example to the world who has not taught it. There is not a philosopher, there is not a religious leader, there is not a creed that has not taught it. This is a Christian community, so-called, at least it boasts of it, and yet they would hang these boys in a Christian community. Let me ask this court, is there any doubt about whether these boys would be safe in the hands of the founder of the Christian religion? It would be blasphemy to say they would not. Nobody could imagine, nobody could even think of it. And yet there are men who want to hang them for a childish, purposeless act, conceived without the slightest malice in the world.

Your Honor, I feel like apologizing for urging it so long. It is not because I doubt this court. It is not because I do not know something of the human emotions and the human heart. It is not that I do not know that every result of logic, every page of history, every line of philosophy and religion, every precedent in this court, urges this court to save life. It is not that. I have become obsessed with this deep feeling of hate and anger that has swept across this city and this land. I have been fighting it, battling with it, until it has fairly driven me mad, until I sometimes

wonder whether every religious human emotion has not gone down in the raging storm.

I am not pleading so much for these boys as I am for the infinite number of others to follow, those who perhaps cannot be as well defended as these have been, those who may go down in the storm and the tempest without aid. It is of them that I am thinking, and for them I am begging of this court not to turn backward toward the barbarous and cruel past.

Now, Your Honor, who are these boys?

Leopold, with a wonderfully brilliant mind; Loeb, with an unusual intelligence; both from their very youth crowded like hothouse plants to learn more and more and more. Dr. Krohn says that they are intelligent. But it takes something besides brains to make a human being who can adjust himself to life.

Brains are not the chief essential in human conduct. The emotions are the urge that makes us live; the urge that makes us work or play, or move along the pathways of life. They are the instinctive things. In fact, intellect is a late development in life. Long before it was evolved, the emotional life kept the organism in existence until death. Whatever our action is, it comes from the emotions, and nobody is balanced without them.

The question of intellect means the smallest part of life. Back of this are man's nerves, muscles, heart, blood, lungs—in fact, the whole organism; the brain is the least part in human development. Without the emotion-life man is nothing. How is it with these two boys? Is there any question about them?

I insist there is not the slightest question about it. All teaching and all training appeals, not only to the intellectual, but to emotional life. A child is born with no ideas of right and wrong, just with plastic brain, ready for such impressions as come to him, ready to be developed. Lying, stealing, killing are not wrong to the child. These mean nothing.

Gradually his parents and his teachers tell him things, teach him habits, show him that he may do this and he may not do that, teach him the difference between his and mine. No child knows this when he is born. He knows nothing about property or property rights. They are given to him as he goes along. He is like the animal that wants something and goes out and gets it, kills it, operating purely from instinct, without training.

The child is gradually taught, and habits are built up. These habits are supposed to be strong enough so that they will form inhibitions against conduct when the emotions come in conflict with the duties of life. Dr. Singer and Dr. Church, both of them, admitted exactly what I am saying now. The child of himself knows nothing about right and wrong, and the teaching built up gives him habits, so he will be able to control certain instincts that surge upon him, and which surge upon everyone who lives. If the instinct is strong enough and the habit weak enough, the habit goes down before it. Both of these eminent men admit it. There can be no question about it. His conduct depends upon the relative strength of the instinct and the habit that has been built up.

Education means fixing these habits so deeply in the life of man that they stand in stead when he needs them to keep him in the path—and that is all it does mean. Suppose one sees a thousand-dollar bill and nobody present.

He may have the impulse to take it. If he does not take it, it will be because his emotional nature revolts at it, through habit and through training. If the emotional nature does not revolt at it he will do it. That is why people do not commit what we call crime; that, and caution. All education means is the building of habits so that certain conduct revolts you and stops you, saves you; but without an emotional nature you cannot do that. Some are born practically without it.

How about this case?

The State put on three alienists and Dr. Krohn. Two of them, Dr. Patrick and Dr. Church, are undoubtedly able men. One of them, Dr. Church, is a man whom I have known for thirty years, and for whom I have the highest regard.

On Sunday, June first, before any of the friends of these boys or their counsel could see them, while they were in the care of the state's attorney's office, they brought them in to be examined by these alienists. I am not going to discuss that in detail as I may later on. Dr. Patrick said that the only thing unnatural he noted about it was that they had no emotional reactions. Dr. Church said the same. These are their alienists, not ours. These boys could tell this gruesome story without a change of countenance, without the slightest feelings. There were no emotional reactions to it. What was the reason? I do not know. How can I tell why? I know what causes the emotional life. I know it comes from the nerves, the muscles, the endocrine glands, the vegetative system. I know it is the most important part of life. I know it is practically left out of some. I know that without it men cannot live. I know that without it they cannot act with the rest. I know they cannot feel what you feel and what I feel; that they cannot feel the

moral shocks which come to men who are educated and who have not been deprived of an emotional system or emotional feelings. I know it, and every person who has honestly studied this subject knows it as well. Is Dickie Loeb to blame because out of the infinite forces that conspired to form him, the infinite forces that were at work producing him ages before he was born, that because out of these infinite combinations he was born without it? If he is, then there should be a new definition for justice. Is he to blame for what he did not have and never had? Is he to blame that his machine is imperfect? Who is to blame? I do not know. I have never in my life been interested so much in fixing blame as I have in relieving people from blame. I am not wise enough to fix it. I know that somewhere in the past that entered into him something missed. It may be defective nerves. It may be a defective heart or liver. It may be defective endocrine glands. I know it is something. I know that nothing happens in this world without a cause.

I know, Your Honor, that if you, sitting here in this court, and in this case, had infinite knowledge, you could lay your fingers on it, and I know you would not visit it on Dickie Loeb. I asked Dr. Church and I asked Dr. Singer whether, if they were wise enough to know, they could not find the cause, and both of them said yes. I know that they and Loeb are just as they are, and that they did not make themselves. There are at least two theories of man's responsibility. There may be more. There is an old theory that if a man does something it is because he willfully, purposely, maliciously, and with a malignant heart sees fit to do it. And that goes back to the possession of man by devils. The old indictments used to read that a man being possessed of a devil did so and so. But why was he

possessed with the devil? Did he invite him in? Could he help it?

Very few half-civilized people believe that doctrine any more. Science has been at work, humanity has been at work, scholarship has been at work, and intelligent people now know that every human being is the product of the endless heredity back of him and the infinite environment around him. He is made as he is and he is the sport of all that goes before him and is applied to him, and under the same stress and storm you would act one way and I another, and poor Dickie Loeb another.

Dr. Church said so and Dr. Singer said so, and it is the truth. Take a normal boy, Your Honor. Do you suppose he could have taken a boy into an automobile without any reason and hit him over the head and killed him? I might just as well ask you whether you thought the sun could shine at midnight in this latitude. It is not a part of normality. Something was wrong.

I am asking Your Honor not to visit the grave and dire and terrible misfortunes of Dickie Loeb and Nathan Leopold upon these two boys. I do not know where to place it. I know it is somewhere in the infinite economy of nature, and if I were wise enough I could find it. I know it is there, and to say that because they are as they are you should hang them, is brutality and cruelty, and savors of the fang and claw.

There can be no question on the evidence in this case. Dr. Church and Dr. Patrick both testified that these boys have no emotional reactions in reference to this crime. Every one of the alienists on both sides has told this court what no doubt this court already knew, that the emotions furnish the urge and the drive to life. A man can get along

without his intellect, and most people do, but he cannot get along without his emotions. When they did make a brain for man, they did not make it good enough to hurt, because emotions can still hold sway. He eats and he drinks, he works and plays and sleeps, in obedience to his emotional system. The intellectual part of man acts only as a judge over his emotions, and then he generally gets it wrong, and has to rely on his instincts to save him.

These boys—I do not care what their mentality; that simply makes it worse—are emotionally defective. Every single alienist who has testified in this case has said so. The only person who did not was Dr. Krohn. While I am on that subject, lest I forget the eminent doctor, I want to refer to one or two things. In the first place, all these alienists that the State called came into the state's attorney's office and heard these boys tell their story of this crime; and that is all they heard.

Now, Your Honor is familiar with Chicago the same as I am, and I am willing to admit right here and now that the two ablest alienists in Chicago are Dr. Church and Dr. Patrick. There may be abler ones, but we lawyers do not know them.

And I will go further: If my friend Crowe had not got to them first, I would have tried to get them. There is no question about it at all. I said I would have tried to; I didn't say I would, and yet I suspect I would. And I say that, Your Honor, without casting the slightest reflection on either one of them, for I really have a high regard for them, and aside from that a deep friendship for Dr. Church. And I have considerable regard for Dr. Singer. I will go no further now.

We could not get them, and Mr. Crowe was very wise, and he deserves a great deal of credit for the industry, the research and the thoroughness that he and his staff have used in detecting this terrible crime.

He worked with intelligence and rapidity. If here and there he trampled on the edges of the Constitution I am not going to talk about it here. If he did it, he is not the first one in that office and probably will not be the last who will do it, so let that go. A great many people in this world believe the end justifies the means. I don't know but that I do myself. And that is the reason I never want to take the side of the prosecution, because I might harm an individual. I am sure the State will live anyhow.

Before the defense had a chance, the State got in two alienists, Church and Patrick, and also called Dr. Krohn, and they sat around hearing these boys tell their stories, and that is all.

Your Honor, they were not holding an examination. They were holding an inquest, and nothing else. It has not the slightest reference to, or earmarks of, an examination for sanity. It was just an inquest; a little premature, but still an inquest.

What is the truth about it? What did Patrick say? He said that it was not a good opportunity for examination. What did Church say? He said that it was not a good opportunity for an examination. What did Krohn say? "Fine—a fine opportunity for an examination," the best he had ever heard of, or that ever anybody had, because their souls were stripped naked. Krohn is not an alienist. He is an orator. He said, because their souls were naked to them. Well, if Krohn's was naked, there would not be much to show.

But Patrick and Church said the conditions were unfavorable for an examination, that they never would choose it, that their opportunities were poor. And yet Krohn states the contrary—Krohn, who by his own admissions, for sixteen years has not been a physician, but has used a license for the sake of haunting these courts, civil and criminal, and going up and down the land peddling perjury.

Your Honor, the mind, of course, is an illusive thing. Whether it exists or not no one can tell. It cannot be found as you find the brain. Its relation to the brain and the nervous system is uncertain. It simply means the activity of the body, which is coordinated with the brain. But when we do find from human conduct that we believe there is a diseased mind, we naturally speculate on how it came about. And we wish to find always, if possible, the reason why it is so. We may find it; we may not find it; because the unknown is infinitely wider and larger than the known, both as to the human mind and as to almost everything else in the universe.

I have tried to study the lives of these two most unfortunate boys. Three months ago, if their friends and the friends of the family had been asked to pick out the most promising lads of their acquaintance, they probably would have picked these two boys. With every opportunity, with plenty of wealth, they would have said that those two would succeed.

In a day, by an act of madness, all this is destroyed, until the best they can hope for now is a life of silence and pain, continuing to the end of their years.

How did it happen?

Let us take Dickie Loeb first.

I do not claim to know how it happened; I have sought to find out. I know that something, or some combinations of things, is responsible for this mad act. I know that there are no accidents in nature. I know that effect follows cause. I know that, if I were wise enough, and knew enough about this case, I could lay my finger on the cause. I will do the best I can, but it is largely speculation.

The child, of course, is born without knowledge.

Impressions are made upon its mind as it goes along. Dickie Loeb was a child of wealth and opportunity. Over and over in this court Your Honor has been asked, and other courts have been asked, to consider boys who have no chance; they have been asked to consider the poor, whose home had been the street, with no education and no opportunity in life, and they have done it, and done it rightfully.

But, Your Honor, it is just as often a great misfortune to be the child of the rich as it is to be the child of the poor. Wealth has its misfortunes. Too much, too great opportunity and advantage, given to a child has its misfortunes, and I am asking Your Honor to consider the rich as well as the poor (and nothing else). Can I find what was wrong? I think I can. Here was a boy at a tender age, placed in the hands of a governess, intellectual, vigorous, devoted, with a strong ambition for the welfare of this boy. He was pushed in his studies, as plants are forced in hothouses. He had no pleasures, such as a boy should have, except as they were gained by lying and cheating.

Now, I am not criticizing the nurse. I suggest that some day Your Honor look at her picture. It explains her fully. Forceful, brooking no interference, she loved the boy, and her ambition was that he should reach the highest perfec-

tion. No time to pause, no time to stop from one book to another, no time to have those pleasures which a boy ought to have to create a normal life. And what happened? Your Honor, what would happen? Nothing strange or unusual. This nurse was with him all the time, except when he stole out at night, from two to fourteen years of age. He, scheming and planning as healthy boys would do, to get out from under her restraint; she, putting before him the best books, which children generally do not want; and he, when she was not looking, reading detective stories, which he devoured, story after story, in his young life. Of all this there can be no question.

What is the result? Every story he read was a story of crime. We have a statute in this state, passed only last year, if I recall it, which forbids minors reading stories of crime. Why? There is only one reason. Because the legislature in its wisdom felt that it would produce criminal tendencies in the boys who read them. The legislature of this state has given its opinion, and forbidden boys to read these books. He read them day after day. He never stopped. While he was passing through college at Ann Arbor he was still reading them. When he was a senior he read them, and almost nothing else.

Now, these facts are beyond dispute. He early developed the tendency to mix with crime, to be a detective; as a little boy shadowing people on the street; as a little child going out with his fantasy of being the head of a band of criminals and directing them on the street. How did this grow and develop in him? Let us see. It seems to be as natural as the day following the night. Every detective story is a story of a sleuth getting the best of it: trailing some unfortunate individual through devious ways until his victim is finally landed in jail or stands on the gallows.

They all show how smart the detective is, and where the criminal himself falls down.

This boy early in his life conceived the idea that there could be a perfect crime, one that nobody could ever detect; that there could be one where the detective did not land his game—a perfect crime. He had been interested in the story of Charley Ross, who was kidnaped. He was interested in these things all his life. He believed in his childish way that a crime could be so carefully planned that there would be no detection, and his idea was to plan and accomplish a perfect crime. It would involve kidnaping and involve murder.

There had been growing in Dickie's brain, dwarfed and twisted—as every act in this case shows it to have been dwarfed and twisted—there had been growing this scheme, not due to any wickedness of Dickie Loeb, for he is a child. It grew as he grew; it grew from those around him; it grew from the lack of the proper training until it possessed him. He believed he could beat the police. He believed he could plan the perfect crime. He had thought of it and talked of it for years—had talked of it as a child, had worked at it as a child—this sorry act of his, utterly irrational and motiveless, a plan to commit a perfect crime which must contain kidnaping, and there must be ransom, or else it could not be perfect, and they must get the money.

The State itself in opening this case said that it was largely for experience and for a thrill, which it was. In the end the State switched it onto the foolish reason of getting cash.

Every fact in this case shows that cash had almost nothing to do with it, except as a factor in the perfect crime;

and to commit the perfect crime there must be a kidnaping, and a kidnaping where they could get money, and that was all there was of it. Now, these are the two theories of this case, and I submit, Your Honor, under the facts in this case, that there can be no question but that we are right. This fantasy grew in the mind of Dickie Loeb almost before he began to read. It developed as a child just as kleptomania has developed in many a person and is clearly recognized by the courts. He went from one thing to another—in the main insignificant, childish things. Then, the utterly foolish and stupid and unnecessary thing of going to Ann Arbor to steal from a fraternity house, a fraternity of which he was a member. And, finally, the planning for this crime. Murder was the least part of it; to kidnap and get the money, and kill in connection with it— that was the childish scheme growing up in these childish minds. And they had it in mind for five or six months— planning what? Planning where every step was foolish and childish; acts that could have been planned in an hour or a day; planning this, and then planning that, changing this and changing that; the weird actions of two mad brains.

Counsel have laughed at us for talking about fantasies and hallucinations. They had laughed at us in one breath, but admitted in another. Let us look at that for a moment, Your Honor. Your Honor has been a child. I well remember that I have been a child. And while youth has its advantages, it has its grievous troubles. There is an old prayer, "Though I grow old in years, let me keep the heart of a child." The heart of a child—with its abundant life, its disregard for consequences, its living in the moment, and for the moment alone, its lack of responsibility, and its freedom from care.

The law knows and has recognized childhood for many and many a long year. What do we know about childhood? The brain of the child is the home of dreams, of castles, of visions, of illusions and of delusions. In fact, there could be no childhood without delusions, for delusions are always more alluring than facts. Delusions, dreams and hallucinations are a part of the warp and woof of childhood. You know it and I know it. I remember, when I was a child, the men seemed as tall as the trees, the trees as tall as the mountains. I can remember very well when, as a little boy, I swam the deepest spot in the river for the first time. I swam breathlessly and landed with as much sense of glory and triumph as Julius Caesar felt when he led his army across the Rubicon. I have been back since, and I can almost step across the same place, but it seemed an ocean then. And those men whom I thought so wonderful were dead and left nothing behind. I had lived in a dream. I had never known the real world which I met, to my discomfort and despair, and that dispelled the illusions of my youth.

The whole life of childhood is a dream and an illusion, and whether they take one shape or another shape depends not upon the dreamy boy but on what surrounds him. As well might I have dreamed of burglars and wished to be one as to dream of policemen and wished to be one. Perhaps I was lucky, too, that I had no money. We have grown to think that the misfortune is in not having it. The great misfortune in this terrible case is the money. That has destroyed their lives. That has fostered these illusions. That has promoted this mad act. And, if Your Honor shall doom them to die, it will be because they are the sons of the rich.

Do you suppose that if they lived up here on the Northwest Side and had no money; with the evidence as clear in this case as it is, that any human being would want to hang them? Excessive wealth is a grievous misfortune in every step in life. When I hear foolish people, when I read malicious newspapers talking of excessive fees in this case, it makes me ill. That there is nothing bigger in life, that it is presumed that no man lives to whom money is not the first concern, than human instincts, sympathy and kindness and charity and logic can only be used for cash. It shows how deeply money has corrupted the hearts of most men.

Now, to get back to Dickie Loeb. He was a child. The books he read by day were not the books he read by night. We are all of us molded somewhat by the influences around us, and of those, to people who read, perhaps books are the greatest and the strongest influences.

I know where my life has been molded by books, amongst other things. We all know where our lives have been influenced by books. The nurse, strict and jealous and watchful, gave him one kind of book; by night he would steal off and read the other.

Which, think you, shaped the life of Dickie Loeb? Is there any kind of question about it? A child. Was it pure maliciousness? Was a boy of five or six or seven to blame for it? Where did he get it? He got it where we all get our ideas, and these books became a part of his dreams and a part of his life, and as he grew up his visions grew to hallucinations.

He went out on the street and fantastically directed his companions, who were not there, in their various moves

to complete the perfect crime. Can there be any sort of question about it?

Suppose, Your Honor, that instead of this boy being here in this court, under the plea of the State that Your Honor shall pronounce a sentence to hang him by the neck until dead, he had been taken to pathological hospital to be analyzed, and the physicians had inquired into his case. What would they have said? There is only one thing that they could possibly have said. They would have traced everything back to the gradual growth of the child.

That is not all there is about it. Youth is hard enough. The only good thing about youth is that it has no thought and no care; and how blindly we can do things when we are young!

Where is the man who has not been guilty of delinquencies in youth? Let us be honest with ourselves. Let us look into our own hearts. How many men are there today—lawyers and congressmen and judges, and even state's attorneys—who have not been guilty of some mad act in youth? And if they did not get caught, or the consequences were trivial, it was their good fortune.

We might as well be honest with ourselves, Your Honor. Before I would tie a noose around the neck of a boy I would try to call back into my mind the emotions of youth. I would try to remember what the world looked like to me when I was a child. I would try to remember how strong were these instinctive, persistent emotions that moved my life. I would try to remember how weak and inefficient was youth in the presence of the surging, controlling feelings of the child. One that honestly remembers and asks himself the question and tries to un-

lock the door he thinks is closed, and calls back the boy, can understand the boy.

But, Your Honor, that is not all there is to boyhood. Nature is strong and she is pitiless. She works in her own mysterious way, and we are her victims. We have not much to do with it ourselves. Nature takes this job in hand, and we play our parts. In the words of old Omar Khayyam, we are only:

But helpless pieces in the game He plays

Upon this checkerboard of nights and days;

Hither and thither moves, and checks, and slays,

And one by one back in the closet lays.

What had this boy to do with it? He was not his own father; he was not his own mother; he was not his own grandparents. All of this was handed to him. He did not surround himself with governesses and wealth. He did not make himself. And yet he is to be compelled to pay.

There was a time in England, running down as late as the beginning of the last century, when judges used to convene court and call juries to try a horse, a dog, a pig, for crime. I have in my library a story of a judge and jury and lawyers trying and convicting an old sow for lying down on her ten pigs and killing them.

What does it mean? Animals were tried. Do you mean to tell me that Dickie Loeb had any more to do with his making than any other product of heredity that is born upon the earth?

Classics of the Courtroom

At this period of life it is not enough to take a boy—Your Honor, I wish I knew when to stop talking about this question that has always interested me so much—it is not enough to take a boy filled with his dreams and his fantasies and living in an unreal world, but the age of adolescence comes on him with all the rest.

What does he know? Both these boys are in the adolescent age. Both these boys, as every alienist in his case on both sides tells you, are in the most trying period of the life of a child—both these boys, when the call of sex is new and strange; both these boys, at a time of seeking to adjust their young lives to the world, moved by the strongest feelings and passions that have ever moved men; both these boys, at the time boys grow insane, at the time crimes are committed. All of this is added to all the rest of the vagaries of their lives. Shall we charge them with full responsibility that we may have a hanging? That we may deck Chicago in a holiday garb and let the people have their fill of blood; that you may put stains upon the heart of every man, woman and child on that day, and that the dead walls of Chicago will tell the story of the shedding of their blood?

For God's sake, are we crazy? In the face of history, of every line of philosophy, against the teaching of every religionist and seer and prophet the world has ever given us, we are still doing what our barbaric ancestors did when they came out of the caves and the woods.

From the age of fifteen to the age of twenty or twenty-one, the child has the burden of adolescence, of puberty and sex thrust upon him. Girls are kept at home and carefully watched. Boys without instruction are left to work the period out for themselves. It may lead to excess. It

may lead to disgrace. It may lead to perversion. Who is to blame? Who did it? Did Dickie Loeb do it?

Your Honor, I am almost ashamed to talk about it. I can hardly imagine that we are in the twentieth century. And yet there are men who seriously say that for what nature has done, for what life has done, for what training has done, you should hang these boys.

Now, there is no mystery about this case, Your Honor. I seem to be criticizing their parents. They had parents who were kind and good and wise in their way. But I say to you seriously that the parents are more responsible than these boys. And yet few boys had better parents.

Your Honor, it is the easiest thing in the world to be a parent. We talk of motherhood, and yet every woman can be a mother. We talk of fatherhood, and yet every man can be a father. Nature takes care of that. It is easy to be a parent. But to be wise and farseeing enough to understand the boy is another thing; only a very few are so wise and so farseeing as that. When I think of the light way nature has of picking our parents and populating the earth, having them born and die, I cannot hold human beings to the same degree of responsibility that young lawyers hold them when they are enthusiastic in a prosecution. I know what it means.

I know there are no better citizens in Chicago than the fathers of these poor boys. I know there were no better women than their mothers. But I am going to be honest with this court, if it is at the expense of both. I know that one of two things happened to Richard Loeb: that this terrible crime was inherent in his organism, and came from some ancestor; or that it came through his education and his training after he was born. Do I need to prove it? Judge

Crowe said at one point in this case, when some witness spoke about their wealth, that "probably that was responsible."

To believe that any boy is responsible for himself or his early training is an absurdity that no lawyer or judge should be guilty of today. Somewhere this came to the boy. If his failing came from his heredity, I do not know where or how. None of us are bred perfect and pure; and the color of our hair, the color of our eyes, our stature, the weight and fineness of our brain, and everything about us could, with full knowledge, be traced with absolute certainty to somewhere. If we had the pedigree it could be traced just the same in a boy as it could in a dog, a horse or a cow.

I do not know what remote ancestors may have sent down the seed that corrupted him, and I do not know through how many ancestors it may have passed until it reached Dickie Loeb.

All I know is that it is true, and there is not a biologist in the world who will not say that I am right.

If it did not come that way, then I know that if he was normal, if he had been understood, if he had been trained as he should have been it would not have happened. Not that anybody may not slip, but I know it and Your Honor knows it, and every schoolhouse and every church in the land is an evidence of it. Else why build them?

Every effort to protect society is an effort toward training the youth to keep the path. Every bit of training in the world proves it, and it likewise proves that it sometimes fails. I know that if this boy had been understood and properly trained—properly for him—and the training that he got might have been the very best for someone; but if

it had been the proper training for him he would not be in this courtroom today with the noose above his head. If there is responsibility anywhere, it is back of him; somewhere in the infinite number of his ancestors, or in his surroundings, or in both. And I submit, Your Honor, that under every principle of natural justice, under every principle of conscience, of right, and of law, he should not be made responsible for the acts of someone else.

I say this again, without finding fault with his parents, for whom I have the highest regard, and who doubtless did the best they could. They might have done better if they had not had so much money. I do not know. Great wealth often curses all who touch it.

This boy was sent to school. His mind worked; his emotions were dead. He could learn books, but he read detective stories. There never was a time since he was old enough to move back and forth, according to what seemed to be his volition, when he was not haunted by these fantasies.

The State made fun of Dr. White, the ablest and, I believe, the best psychiatrist in America today, for speaking about this boy's mind running back to the Teddy bears he used to play with, and in addressing somebody he was wont to say, "You know, Teddy—"

Well, Your Honor, is it nothing but the commonplace action of the commonplace child or the ordinary man? A set of emotions, thoughts, feelings take possession of the mind and we find them recurring and recurring over and over again.

I catch myself many and many a time repeating phrases of my childhood, and I have not quite got into my second childhood yet. I have caught myself doing this while I still

could catch myself. It means nothing. We may have all the dreams and visions and build all the castles we wish, but the castles of youth should be discarded with youth, and when they linger to the time when boys should think wiser things, then it indicates a diseased mind.

"When I was young, I thought as a child, I spoke as a child, I understood as a child; but now I have put off childish things," said the Psalmist twenty centuries ago.

It is when these dreams of boyhood, these fantasies of youth still linger, and the growing boy is still a child—a child in emotion, a child in feeling, a child in hallucinations—that you can say that it is the dreams and the hallucinations of childhood that are responsible for his conduct. There is not an act in all this horrible tragedy that was not the act of a child, the act of a child wandering around in the morning of life, moved by the new feelings of a boy, moved by the uncontrolled impulses which his teaching was not strong enough to take care of, moved by the dreams and the hallucinations which haunt the brain of a child. I say, Your Honor, that it would be the height of cruelty, of injustice, of wrong and barbarism to visit the penalty upon this poor boy.

Your Honor, again I want to say that all parents can be criticized; likewise grandparents and teachers. Science is not so much interested in criticism as in finding causes. Sometime education will be more scientific. Sometime we will try to know the boy before we educate and as we educate him. Sometime we will try to know what will fit the individual boy, instead of putting all boys through the same course, regardless of what they are.

This boy needed more of home, more love, more directing. He needed to have his emotions awakened. He

needed guiding hands along the serious road that youth must travel. Had these been given him, he would not be here today.

Now, Your Honor, I want to speak of the other lad, Babe.

Babe is somewhat older than Dick, and is a boy of remarkable mind -- away beyond his years. He is a sort of freak in this direction, as in others; a boy without emotions, a boy obsessed of philosophy, a boy obsessed of learning, busy every minute of his life.

He went through school quickly; he went to college young; he could learn faster than almost everybody else. his emotional life was lacking, as every alienist and witness in this case, excepting Dr. Krohn has told you. He was just a half-boy, an intellect, an intellectual machine going without balance and without a governor, seeking to find out everything there was in life intellectually; seeking to solve every philosophy by using his intellect only.

Of course his family did not understand him; few men would. His mother died when he was young; he had plenty of money; everything was given to him that he wanted. Both these boys with unlimited money; both these boys with automobiles; both these boys with every luxury around them and in front of them. They grew up in this environment.

Babe took up philosophy. I call him Babe, not because I want it to affect Your Honor, but because everybody else does. He is the youngest of the family and I suppose that is why he got his nickname. We will call him a man. Mr. Crowe thinks it is easier to hang a man than a boy, and so I will call him a man if I can think of it.

He grew up in this way. He became enamored of the philosophy of Nietzsche.

Your Honor, I have read almost everything that Nietzsche ever wrote. He was a man of a wonderful intellect; the most original philosopher of the last century. A man who probably has made a deeper imprint on philosophy than any other man in a hundred years, whether right or wrong. More books have been written about him than probably all the rest of the philosophers in a hundred years. More college professors have talked about him. In a way he has reached more people, and still he has been a philosopher of what we might call the intellectual cult. Nietzsche believed that some time the superman would be born, that evolution was working toward the superman.

He wrote one book, *Beyond Good and Evil,* which was a criticism of all moral codes as the world understands them; a treatise holding that the intelligent man is beyond good and evil; that the laws for good and the laws for evil do not apply to those who approach the superman. He wrote on the will to power. He wrote some ten or fifteen volumes on his various philosophical ideas. Nathan Leopold is not the only boy who has read Nietzsche. He may be the only one who was influenced in the way that he was influenced.

It is not how he would affect you. It is not how he would affect me. The question is how he did affect the impressionable, visionary, dreamy mind of a boy.

At seventeen, at sixteen, at eighteen, while healthy boys were playing baseball or working on the farm or doing odd jobs, he was reading Nietzsche, a boy who never should have seen it at that early age. Babe was ob-

sessed of it, and here are some of the things which Nietzsche taught:

"Why so soft, oh, my brethren? Why so soft, so unresisting and yielding? Why is there so much disavowal and abnegation in your heart? Why is there so little fate in your looks? For all creators are hard, and it must seem blessedness unto you to press your hand upon millenniums and upon wax. This new table, oh, my brethren, I put over you: Become hard. To be obsessed by moral consideration presupposes a very low grade of intellect. We should substitute for morality the will to our own end, and consequently to the means to accomplish that.

"A great man, a man that nature has built up and invented in a grand style, is colder, harder, less cautious and more free from the fear of public opinion. He does not possess the virtues which are compatible with respectability, with being respected, nor any of those things which are counted among the virtues of the hard."

Nietzsche held a contemptuous, scornful attitude to all those things which the young are taught as important in life; a fixing of new values which are not the values by which any normal child has ever yet been reared—a philosophical dream, containing more or less truth, that was not meant by anyone to be applied to life.

Again he says:

"The morality of the master class is irritating to the taste of the present day because of its fundamental principle that a man has obligation only to his equals; that he may act to all of lower rank and to all that are foreign, as he pleases."

In other words, man has no obligations; he may do with all other men and all other boys, and all society, as he pleases—the superman was a creation of Nietzsche, but it has permeated every college and university in the civilized world.

Quoting from a professor of a university:

"Although no perfect superman has yet appeared in history, Nietzsche's types are to be found in the world's great figures—Alexander, Napoleon—in the wicked heroes such as the Borgias, Wagner's Siegfried and Ibsen's Brand—and the great cosmopolitan intellects such as Goethe and Stendahl. These were the gods of Nietzsche's idolatry.

"The superman-like qualities lie not in their genius, but in their freedom from scruple. They rightly felt themselves to be above the law. What they thought was right, not because sanctioned by any law, beyond themselves, but because they did it. So the superman will be a law unto himself. What he does will come from the will and superabundant power within him."

Your Honor, I could read for a week about Nietzsche, all to the same purpose, and the same end.

Counsel have said that because a man believes in murder that does not excuse him.

Quite right. But this is not a case like the anarchists' case, where a number of men, perhaps honestly believing in revolution and knowing the consequences of their act and knowing its illegal character, were held responsible for murder.

Of course the books are full of statements that the fact that a man believes in committing a crime does not excuse him.

That is not this case, and counsel must know that it is not this case. Here is a boy at sixteen or seventeen becoming obsessed with these doctrines. There isn't any question about the facts. Their own witnesses tell it and every one of our witnesses tell it. It was not a casual bit of philosophy with him; it was his life. He believed in a superman. He and Dickie Loeb were the supermen. There might have been others, but they were two, and two chums. The ordinary commands of society were not for him.

Many of us read this philosophy but know that it has no actual application to life; but not he. It became a part of his being. It was his philosophy. He lived it and practiced it; he thought it applied to him, and he could not have believed it excepting that it either caused a diseased mind or was the result of a diseased mind.

Now let me call your attention hastily to just a few facts in connection with it. One of the cases is a New York case, where a man named Freeman became obsessed in a very strange way of religious ideas. He read the story of Isaac and Abraham and he felt a call that he must sacrifice his son. He arranged an altar in his parlor. He converted his wife to the idea. He took his little babe and put it on the altar and cut its throat. Why? Because he was obsessed of that idea. Was he sane? Was he normal? Was his mind diseased? Was this poor fellow responsible? Not in the least. And he was acquitted because he was the victim of a delusion. Men are largely what their ideas make them. Boys largely what their ideas make them.

Here is a boy who by day and by night, in season and out, was talking of the superman, owing no obligations to anyone; whatever gave him pleasure he should do, believing it just as another man might believe a religion or any philosophical theory.

You remember that I asked Dr. Church about these religious cases and he said, "Yes, many people go to the insane asylum on account of them," that "They place a literal meaning on parables and believe them thoroughly." I asked Dr. Church, whom I again say I believe to be an honest man, and an intelligent man—I asked him whether the same thing might be done or might come from a philosophical belief, and he said, "If one believed it strongly enough."

And I asked him about Nietzsche. He said he knew something of Nietzsche, something of his responsibility for the war, for which he perhaps was not responsible. He said he knew something about his doctrines. I asked him what became of him, and he said he was insane for fifteen years just before the time of his death. His very doctrine is a species of insanity.

Here is a man, a wise man—perhaps not wise, but brilliant—a thoughtful man who has made his impress upon the world. Every student of philosophy knows him. His own doctrines made him a maniac. And here is a young boy, in the adolescent age, harassed by everything that harasses children, who takes this philosophy and believes it literally. It is a part of his life. It is his life. Do you suppose this mad act could have been done by him in any other way? What could he have to win from this homicide?

A boy with a beautiful home, with automobiles, a graduate of college, going to Europe, and then to study law at Harvard; as brilliant in intellect as any boy that you could find; a boy with every prospect that life might hold out to him; and yet he goes out and commits this weird, strange, wild, mad act, that he may die on the gallows or live in a prison cell until he dies of old age or disease.

He did it, obsessed of an idea, perhaps to some extent influenced by what has not been developed publicly in this case—perversions that were present in the boy. Both signs of insanity; both, together with this act, proving a diseased mind.

Is there any question about what was responsible for him?

What else could be? A boy in his youth, with every promise that the world could hold out before him—wealth and position and intellect, yes, genius, scholarship, nothing that he could not obtain, and he throws it away, and mounts the gallows or goes into a cell for life. It is too foolish to talk about. Can Your Honor imagine a sane brain doing it? Can you imagine it coming from anything but a diseased mind? Can you imagine it is any part of normality? And yet, Your Honor, you are asked to hang a boy of his age, abnormal, obsessed of dreams and visions, a philosophy that destroyed his life, when there is no sort of question in the world as to what caused his downfall.

Now, I have said that, as to Loeb, if there is anybody to blame, it is back of him. Your Honor, lots of things happen in this world that nobody is to blame for. In fact, I am not very much for settling blame myself. If I could settle the blame on somebody else for this special act, I would

wonder why that somebody else did it, and I know if I could find that out, I would move it back still another peg.

I know, Your Honor, that every atom of life in all this universe is bound up together. I know that a pebble cannot be thrown into the ocean without disturbing every drop of water in the sea. I know that every life is inextricably mixed and woven with every other life. I know that every influence, conscious and unconscious, acts and reacts on every living organism, and that no one can fix the blame. I know that all life is a series of infinite chances, which sometimes result one way and sometimes another. I have not the infinite wisdom that can fathom it; neither has any other human brain. But I do know that if back of it is a power that made it, that power alone can tell, and if there is no power, then it is an infinite chance, which man cannot solve.

Why should this boy's life be bound up with Friedrich Nietzsche who died thirty years ago, insane, in Germany? I don't know.

I only know it is. I know that no man who ever wrote a line that I read failed to influence me to some extent. I know that every life I ever touched influenced me, and I influenced it; and that it is not given to me to unravel the infinite causes and say, "This is I, and this is you. I am responsible for so much; and you are responsible for so much." I know—I know that in the infinite universe everything has its place and that the smallest particle is a part of all. Tell me that you can visit the wrath of fate and chance and life and eternity upon a nineteen-year-old boy! If you could, justice would be a travesty and mercy a fraud.

I might say further about Nathan Leopold—where did he get this philosophy?—at college? He did not make it, Your Honor. He did not write these books, and I will venture to say there are at least ten thousand books on Nietzsche and his philosophy. I never counted them, but I will venture to say that there are that many in the libraries of the world.

No other philosopher ever caused the discussion that Nietzsche has caused. There is no university in the world where the professors are not familiar with Nietzsche; not one. There is not an intellectual man in the world whose life and feelings run to philosophy who is not more or less familiar with the Nietzschean philosophy. Some believe it, and some do not believe it. Some read it as I do, and take it as a theory, a dream, a vision, mixed with good and bad, but not in any way related to human life. Some take it seriously. The universities perhaps do not all teach it, for perhaps some teach nothing in philosophy; but they give the boys the books of the masters, and tell them what they taught, and discuss the doctrines.

There is not a university in the world of any high standing where the professors do not tell you about Nietzsche, and discuss it, or where books cannot be found.

I will guarantee that you can go down to the University of Chicago today—into its big library—and find over a thousand volumes on Nietzsche, and I am sure I speak moderately. If this boy is to blame for this, where did he get it? Is there any blame attached because somebody took Nietzsche's philosophy seriously and fashioned his life on it? And there is no question in this case that is true. Then who is to blame? The university would be more to blame than he is. The scholars of the world would be more to blame than he is. The publishers of the world—and

Nietzsche's books are published by one of the biggest publishers in the world—are more to blame than he. Your Honor, it is hardly fair to hang a nineteen-year-old boy for the philosophy that was taught him at the university.

Now, I do not want to be misunderstood about this. Even for the sake of saving the lives of my clients, I do not want to be dishonest and tell the court something that I do not honestly think in this case. I do not believe that the universities are to blame. I do not think they should be held responsible. I do think, however, that they are too large, and that they should keep a closer watch, if possible, upon the individual. But, you cannot destroy thought because, forsooth, some brain may be deranged by thought. It is the duty of the university, as I conceive it, to get the great storehouse of the wisdom of the ages, and to let students go there, and learn, and choose. I have no doubt but that it has meant the death of many; that we cannot help. Every changed idea in the world has had its consequences. Every new religious doctrine has created its victims. Every new philosophy has caused suffering and death. Every new machine has carved up men while it served the world. No railroad can be built without the destruction of human life. No great building can be erected but that unfortunate workmen fall to the earth and die. No great movement that does not bear its toll of life and death; no great ideal but does good and harm, and we cannot stop because it may do harm.

I have no idea in this case that this act would ever have been committed or participated in by him excepting for the philosophy which he had taken literally, which belonged to older boys and older men, and which no one can take literally and practice literally and live. So, Your Honor, I do not mean to unload this act on that man or

this man, or this organization or that organization. I am trying to trace causes. I am trying to trace them honestly. I am trying to trace them with the light I have. I am trying to say to this court that these boys are not responsible for this; and that their act was due to this and this, and this and this; and asking this court not to visit the judgement of its wrath upon them for things for which they are not to blame.

These boys, neither one of them, could possibly have committed this act excepting by coming together. It was not the act of one; it was the act of two. It was the act of their planning, their conniving, their believing in each other; their thinking themselves supermen. Without it they could not have done it. It would not have happened. Their parents happened to meet, these boys happened to meet; some sort of chemical alchemy operated so that they cared for each other, and poor Bobby Franks's dead body was found in a culvert as a result. Neither of them could have done it alone.

I want to call your attention, Your Honor, to the two letters in this case which settle this matter to my mind conclusively; not only the condition of these boys' minds, but the terrible fate that overtook them.

Your Honor, I am sorry for poor Bobby Franks, and I think anybody who knows me knows that I am not saying it simply to talk. I am sorry for the bereaved father and he bereaved mother, and I would like to know what they would do with these poor unfortunate lads who are here in this court today. I know something of them, of their lives, of their charity, of their ideas, and nobody here sympathizes with them more than I.

On the twenty-first day of May poor Bobby Franks, stripped and naked, was left in a culvert down near the Indiana line. I know it came through the act of mad boys. Mr. Savage told us that Franks, if he lived, would have been a great man and have accomplished much. I want to leave this thought with Your Honor now. I do not know what Bobby Franks would have been had he grown to be a man. I do not know the laws that control one's growth. Sometimes, Your Honor, a boy of great promise is cut off in his early youth. Sometimes he dies and is placed in a culvert. Sometimes a boy of great promise stands on a trap door and is hanged by the neck until dead. Sometimes he dies of diphtheria. Death somehow pays no attention to age, sex, prospects, wealth, or intellect.

It comes, and perhaps—I can only say perhaps, for I never professed to unravel the mysteries of fate, and I cannot tell; but I can say perhaps—the boy who died at fourteen did as much as if he had died at seventy, and perhaps the boy who died as a babe did as much as if he had lived longer. Perhaps, somewhere in fate and chance, it might be that he lived as long as he should.

And I want to say this, that the death of poor little Bobby Franks should not be in vain. Would it mean anything if on account of that death, these two boys were taken out and a rope tied around their necks and they died felons? Would that show that Bobby Franks had a purpose in his life and a purpose in his death? No, Your Honor, the unfortunate and tragic death of this young lad should mean something. It should mean an appeal to the fathers and the mothers, an appeal to the teachers, to the religious guides, to society at large. It should mean an appeal to all of them to appraise children, to understand the

emotions that control them, to understand the ideas that possess them, to teach them to avoid the pitfalls of life.

Society, too, should assume its share of the burdens of this case, and not make two more tragedies, but use this calamity as best it can to make life safer, to make childhood easier and more secure, to do something to cure the cruelty, the hatred, the chance, and the willfulness of life.

I have discussed somewhat in detail these two boys separately. Their coming together was the means of their undoing. Your Honor is familiar with the facts in reference to their association. They had a weird, almost impossible relationship. Leopold, with his obsession of the superman, had repeatedly said that Loeb was his idea of the superman. He had the attitude toward him that one has to his most devoted friend, or that a man has to a lover. Without the combination of these two, nothing of this sort probably could have happened.

Now, Your Honor, I shall pass that subject. I think all of the facts of this extraordinary case, all of the testimony of the alienists, all that Your Honor has seen and heard, all their friends and acquaintances who have come here to enlighten this court—I think all of it shows that this terrible act was the act of immature and diseased brains, the act of children.

Nobody can explain it any other way.

No one can imagine it any other way.

It is not possible that it could have happened in any other way.

And, I submit, Your Honor, that by every law of humanity, by every law of justice, by every feeling of

righteousness, by every instinct of pity, mercy and charity, Your Honor should say that because of the condition of these boys' minds, it would be monstrous to visit upon them the vengeance that is asked by the State.

I want to discuss now another thing which this court must consider and which to my mind is absolutely conclusive in this case. That is, the age of these boys.

I shall discuss it in more detail than I have discussed it before, and I submit, Your Honor, that it is not possible for any court to hang these two boys if he pays any attention whatever to the modern attitude toward the young, if he pays any attention whatever to the precedents in this county, if he pays any attention to the humane instincts which move ordinary man.

I have a list of executions in Cook County beginning in 1840, which I presume covers the first one, because I asked to have it go to the beginning. Ninety poor unfortunate men have given up their lives to stop murder in Chicago. Ninety men have been hanged by the neck until dead, because of the ancient superstition that in some way hanging one man keeps another from committing a crime. The ancient superstition, I say, because I defy the State to point to a criminologist, a scientist, a student, who has ever said it. Still we go on, as if human conduct was not influenced and controlled by natural laws the same as all the rest of the universe is the subject of law. We treat crime as if it has no cause. We go on saying, "Hang the unfortunates, and it will end." Was there ever a murder without a cause? And yet all punishment proceeds upon the theory that there is no cause; and the only way to treat crime is to intimidate everyone into goodness and obedience to law. We lawyers are a long way behind.

Crime has its cause. Perhaps all crimes do not have the same cause, but they all have some cause. And people today are seeking to find out the cause. We lawyers never try to find out. Scientists are studying it; criminologists are investigating it; but we lawyers go on and on, punishing and hanging, and thinking that by general terror we can stamp out crime.

It never occurs to the lawyer that crime has a cause as certainly as disease, and that the way to treat any abnormal condition rationally is to remove the cause.

If a doctor were called on to treat typhoid fever he would probably try to find out what kind of milk or water the patient drank, and perhaps clean out the well so that no one else could get typhoid from the same source. But if a lawyer was called on to treat a typhoid patient, he would give him thirty days in jail, and then he would think that nobody else would ever dare to take it. If the patient got well in fifteen days, he would be kept until his time was up; if the disease was worse at the end of thirty days, the patient would be released because his time was out.

As a rule, lawyers are not scientists. They have learned the doctrine of hate and fear, and they think that there is only one way to make men good, and that is to put them in such terror that they do not dare to be bad. They act unmindful of history, and science, and all the experience of the past.

Still, we are making some progress. Courts give attention to some things that they did not give attention to before.

Once in England they hanged children seven years of age; not necessarily hanged them, because hanging was never meant for punishment; it was meant for an exhibi-

tion. If somebody committed crime, he would be hanged by the head or the heels, it didn't matter much which, at the four crossroads, so that everybody could look at him until his bones were bare, and so that people would be good because they had seen the gruesome result of crime and hate.

Hanging was not necessarily meant for punishment. The culprit might be killed in any other way, and then hanged—yes. Hanging was an exhibition. They were hanged on the highest hill, and hanged at the crossroads, and hanged in public places, so that all men could see. If there is any virtue in hanging, that was the logical way, because you cannot awe men into goodness unless they know about the hanging. We have not grown better than the ancients. We have grown more squeamish; we do not like to look at it, that is all. They hanged them at seven years; they hanged them again at eleven and fourteen.

We have raised the age of hanging. We have raised it by the humanity of courts, by the understanding of courts, by the progress in science which is at last reaching the law; and of ninety men hanged in Illinois from its beginning, not one single person under twenty-three was ever hanged upon a plea of guilty—not one. If Your Honor should do this, you would violate every precedent that has been set in Illinois for almost a century. There can be no excuse for it, and no justification for it, because this is the policy of the law which is rooted in the feelings of humanity, which are deep in every human being that thinks and feels. There have been two or three cases where juries have convicted boys younger than this, and where courts on convictions have refused to set aside the sentence. But this was because a jury had decided it.

Clarence Darrow

Your Honor, if in this court a boy of eighteen and a boy of nineteen should be hanged on a plea of Guilty, in violation of every precedent of the past, in violation of the policy of the law to take care of the young, in violation of all the progress that has been made and of all the humanity that has been shown in the care of the young, in violation of the law that places boys in reformatories instead of prisons—if Your Honor, in violation of all that and in the face of all the past, should stand here in Chicago alone to hang a boy on a plea of Guilty, then we are turning our faces backward toward the barbarism which once possessed the world. If Your Honor can hang a boy of eighteen, some other judge can hang him at seventeen, or sixteen, or fourteen. Some day, if there is any such thing as progress in the world, if there is any spirit of humanity that is working in the hearts of men, someday men would look back upon this as a barbarous age which deliberately set itself in the way of progress, humanity and sympathy, and committed an unforgivable act.

Now, Your Honor, I have spoken about the war. I believed in it. I don't know whether I was crazy or not. Sometimes I think perhaps I was. I approved of it; I joined in the general cry of madness and despair. I urged men to fight. I was safe because I was too old to go. I was like the rest. What did they do? Right or wrong, justifiable or unjustifiable—which I need not discuss today—it changed the world. For four long years the civilized world was killing men. Christian against Christian; barbarians uniting with Christians to kill Christians; anything to kill. It was taught in every school, aye in the Sunday schools. The little children played at war. The toddling children on the street. Do you suppose this world has ever been the same since then? How long, Your Honor, will it take for the world to get back the humane emotions that were

slowly growing before the war? How long will it take the calloused hearts of men before the scars of hatred and cruelty shall be removed?

We read of killing one hundred thousand men in a day. We read about it and we rejoiced in it—if it was the other fellows who were killed. We were fed on flesh and drank blood. Even down to the prattling babe. I need not tell Your Honor this, because you know; I need not tell you how many upright, honorable young boys have come into this court charged with murder, some saved and some sent to their death, boys who fought in this war and learned to place a cheap value on human life. You know it and I know it. These boys were brought up in it. The tales of death were in their homes, their playgrounds, their schools; they were in the newspapers that they read; it was a part of the common frenzy. What was a life? It was nothing. It was the least sacred thing in existence and these boys were trained to this cruelty.

It will take fifty years to wipe it out of the human heart, if ever. I know this, that after the Civil War in 1865, crimes of this sort increased marvelously. No one needs to tell me that crime has no cause. It has as definite a cause as any other disease, and I know that out of the hatred and bitterness of the Civil War crime increased as America had never known it before. I know that growing out of the Napoleonic wars there was an era of crime such as Europe had never seen before. I know that Europe is going through the same experience today; I know it has followed every war; and I know it has influenced these boys so that life was not the same to them as it would have been if the world had not been made red with blood. I protest against the crimes and mistakes of society being visited upon them. All of us have our share of it. I have mine. I cannot

tell and I shall never know how many words of mine might have given birth to cruelty in place of love and kindness and charity.

Your Honor knows that in this very court crimes of violence have increased, growing out of the war. Not necessarily by those who fought but by those who learned that blood was cheap, and if the State could take it lightly why not the boy? There are causes for this terrible crime. There are causes, as I have said, for everything that happens in the world. War is a part of it; education is a part of it; birth is a part of it; money is a part of it—all these conspired to compass the destruction of these two poor boys.

Has the court any right to consider anything but these two boys? The State says that Your Honor has a right to consider the welfare of the community, as you have. If the welfare of the community would be benefited by taking these lives, well and good. I think it would work evil that no one could measure. Has Your Honor a right to consider the families of these two defendants? I have been sorry, and I am sorry for the bereavement of Mr. and Mrs. Franks, for those broken ties that cannot be healed. All I can hope and wish is that some good may come from it all. But as compared with the families of Leopold and Loeb, the Franks are to be envied—and everyone knows it.

I do not know how much salvage there is in these two boys. I hate to say it in their presence, but what is there to look forward to? I do not know but that Your Honor would be merciful if you tied a rope around their necks and let them die; merciful to them, but not merciful to civilization, and not merciful to those who would be left behind. To spend the balance of their lives in prison is mighty lit-

tle to look forward to, if anything. Is it anything? They may have the hope that as the years roll around they might be released. I do not know. I do not know. I will be honest with this court as I have tried to be from the beginning. I know that these boys are not fit to be at large. I believe they will not be until they pass through the next stage of life, at forty-five or fifty. Whether they will be then, I cannot tell. I am sure of this; that I will not be here to help them. So far as I am concerned, it is over.

I would not tell this court that I do not hope that some time, when life and age have changed their bodies, as it does, and has changed their emotions, as it does—that they may once more return to life. I would be the last person on earth to close the door to any human being that lives, and least of all to my clients. But what have they to look forward to? Nothing. And I think here of the stanza of Housman:

Now hollow fires burn out to black,

And lights are fluttering low:

Square your shoulders, lift your pack

And leave your friends and go.

O never fear, lads, naught's to dread,

Look not left nor right:

In all the endless road you tread

There's nothing but the night.

I care not, Your Honor, whether the march begins at the gallows or when the gates of Joliet close upon them,

there is nothing but the night, and that is little for any human being to expect.

But there are others to consider. Here are these two families, who have led honest lives, who will bear the name that they bear, and future generations must carry it on.

Here is Leopold's father—and this boy was the pride of his life. He watched him, he cared for him, he worked for him; the boy was brilliant and accomplished, he educated him, and he thought that fame and position awaited him, as it should have awaited. It is a hard thing for a father to see his life's hopes crumble into dust.

Should he be considered? Should his brothers be considered? Will it do society any good or make your life safer, or any human being's life safer, if it should be handed down from generation to generation, that this boy, their kin, died upon the scaffold?

And Loeb's, the same. Here are the faithful uncle and brother, who have watched here by day, while Dickie's father and his mother are too ill to stand this terrific strain, and shall be waiting for a message which means more to them than it can mean to you or me. Shall these be taken into account in this general bereavement?

Have they any rights? Is there any reason, Your Honor, why their proud names and all the future generations that bear them shall have this bar sinister written across them? How many boys and girls, how many unborn children, will feel it? It is bad enough, however it is. But it's not yet death on the scaffold. It's not that. And I ask Your Honor, in addition to all that I have said, to save two honorable families from a disgrace that never ends, and

which could be of no avail to help any human being that lives.

Now, I must say a word more and then I will leave this with you where I should have left it long ago. None of us are unmindful of the public; courts are not, and juries are not. We placed our fate in the hands of a trained court, thinking that he would be more mindful and considerate than a jury. I cannot say how people feel. I have stood here for three months as one might stand at the ocean trying to sweep back the tide. I hope the seas are subsiding and the wind is falling, and I believe they are, but I wish to make no false pretense to this court. The easy thing and the popular thing to do is to hang my clients. I know it. Men and women who do not think will applaud. The cruel and thoughtless will approve. It will be easy today; but in Chicago, and reaching out over the length and breadth of the land, more and more fathers and mothers, the humane, the kind and the hopeful, who are gaining an understanding and asking questions not only about these poor boys, but about their own—these will join in no acclaim at the death of my clients. They would ask that the shedding of blood be stopped, and that the normal feelings of man resume their sway. And as the days and the months and the years go on, they will ask it more and more. But, Your Honor, what they shall ask may not count. I know the easy way. I know Your Honor stands between the future and the past. I know the future is with me, and what I stand for here; not merely for the lives of these two unfortunate lads, but for all boys and girls; for all of the young, and, as far as possible, for all of the old. I am pleading for life, understanding, charity, kindness, and the infinite mercy that considers all. I am pleading that we overcome cruelty with kindness, and hatred with love. I know the future is on my side.

Your Honor stands between the past and the future. You may hang these boys; you may hang them by the neck until they are dead. But in doing it you will turn your face toward the past. In doing it you are making it harder for every other boy who, in ignorance and darkness, must grope his way through the mazes which only childhood knows. In doing it you will make it harder for unborn children. You may save them and make it easier for every child that sometime may stand where these boys stand. You will make it easier for every human being with an aspiration and a vision and a hope and a fate.

I am pleading for the future; I am pleading for a time when hatred and cruelty will not control the hearts of men, when we can learn by reason and judgement and understanding and faith that all life is worth saving, and that mercy is the highest attribute of man.

I feel that I should apologize for the length of time I have taken. This case may not be as important as I think it is, and I am sure I do not need to tell this court, or to tell my friends that I would fight just as hard for the poor as for the rich. If I should succeed in saving these boys' lives and do nothing for the progress of the law, I should feel sad, indeed. If I can succeed, my greatest reward and my greatest hope will be that I have done something for the tens of thousands of other boys, for the countless unfortunates who must tread the same road in blind childhood that these poor boys have trod; that I have done something to help human understanding, to temper justice with mercy, to overcome hate with love.

I was reading last night of the aspiration of the old Persian poet, Omar Khayyam. It appealed to me as the highest that I can vision. I wish it was in my heart, and I wish it was in the hearts of all.

So I be written in the Book of Love,
I do not care about that Book above;
Erase my name or write it as you will,
So I be written in the Book of Love.

Irving Younger 1932 - 1988

The legal profession's greatest advocate of beauty and simplicity passed away on Sunday, March 13, 1988. Irving Younger was the most prolific and respected continuing legal education lecturer of our time. He devoted his professional career to removing the mystery and simplifying the intricacy of the law. Through his teaching, lecturing and writing, he helped tens of thousands of other lawyers and judges practice their craft with enhanced skill, creativity and enthusiasm.

In a career that inspires awe and envy, he served in private practice, as an Assistant United States Attorney, as a Judge in the Civil Court of the City of New York, as a law professor, legal scholar and the most respected continuing legal education lecturer in the country. Blending his uncompromising expertise as a lawyer with elements of science, politics, theatre, art and history, he brought common sense, humanity, grace and charm to an otherwise rigid profession. Irving Younger gave to the law what Mozart did to music, what Shakespere did to theatre and what Michaelangelo did to painting - a special energy that excites our senses and energizes our imaginations.

Students of the craft of advocacy are poorer today for his passing. His great legacy, however, lives on in the countless thousands of law students and lawyers who have been enriched by his boundless love of the law. Our challenge is to rethink the lessons he taught us and rededicate ourselves to the standards of excellence that he defined for us in his brilliant career. Elegance, beauty and simplicity in the practice of law need not, and indeed will not, pass with their greatest proponent. We are all richer for having known him.

CLASSICS OF THE COURTROOM

Series One - Eight Volumes

Max Steuer's Cross Examination of Kate Alterman in
People v. Harris & Blanck and
The Summations of Max Steuer and Joseph M. Proskauer in
Oppenheim v. Metropolitan Street Railways

Robert Hanley's Summation in *MCI v. AT&T I*

Clarence Darrow's Cross Examination of
William Jennings Bryan in
Tennessee v. John Thomas Scopes

Irving Younger's Opening Statement in
Tavoulareas v. The Washington Post Co.

Thomas Murphy's Cross-Examination of
Dr. Carl A. Binger in
United States v. Alger Hiss (Hiss II)

Edward Bennett Williams' Cross-Examination
of Jake Jacobson in *United States v. Connally*

Highlights from the Direct and Cross-Examination of
Herman Goering in *The Nuremberg Trial*

Clarence Darrow's Sentencing Speech in
State of Illinois v. Leopold and Loeb

Series Two - Eight Volumes

James Brosnahan's Summation in
U.S. v. Aguilar (The Sanctuary Trial)

William H. Wallace's Summation in
Missouri v. Frank James

The Direct and Cross-Examination of John Dean
in *U.S. v. Mitchell*

(continued on following page)

Vincent Fuller's Summation in
U.S. v. Hinckley

Highlights from the Direct and Cross-Examination
of Richard Hauptmann in *The State of New Jersey v. Hauptmann*
(The Lindbergh Kidnapping Trial)

Lantz Welch's Summation in
Firestone v. Crown Center Redevelopment Corporation
(Kansas City Hyatt Skywalk Case)

Ulysses in Court (Speech by
Irving Younger)

For a complete listing of continuing legal education
audio tapes, video tapes and manuals contact:

**The Professional Education Group, Inc.
12401 Minnetonka Boulevard
Minnetonka, Minnesota 55343
Phone 612/933-9990**